Frühlings- und Sommerimpressionen von Semmering, Rax, Schneeberg und Wechsel bis in die Bucklige Welt

Spring- and Summerimpressions from Semmering, Rax, Schneeberg and Wechsel to the Bucklige Welt

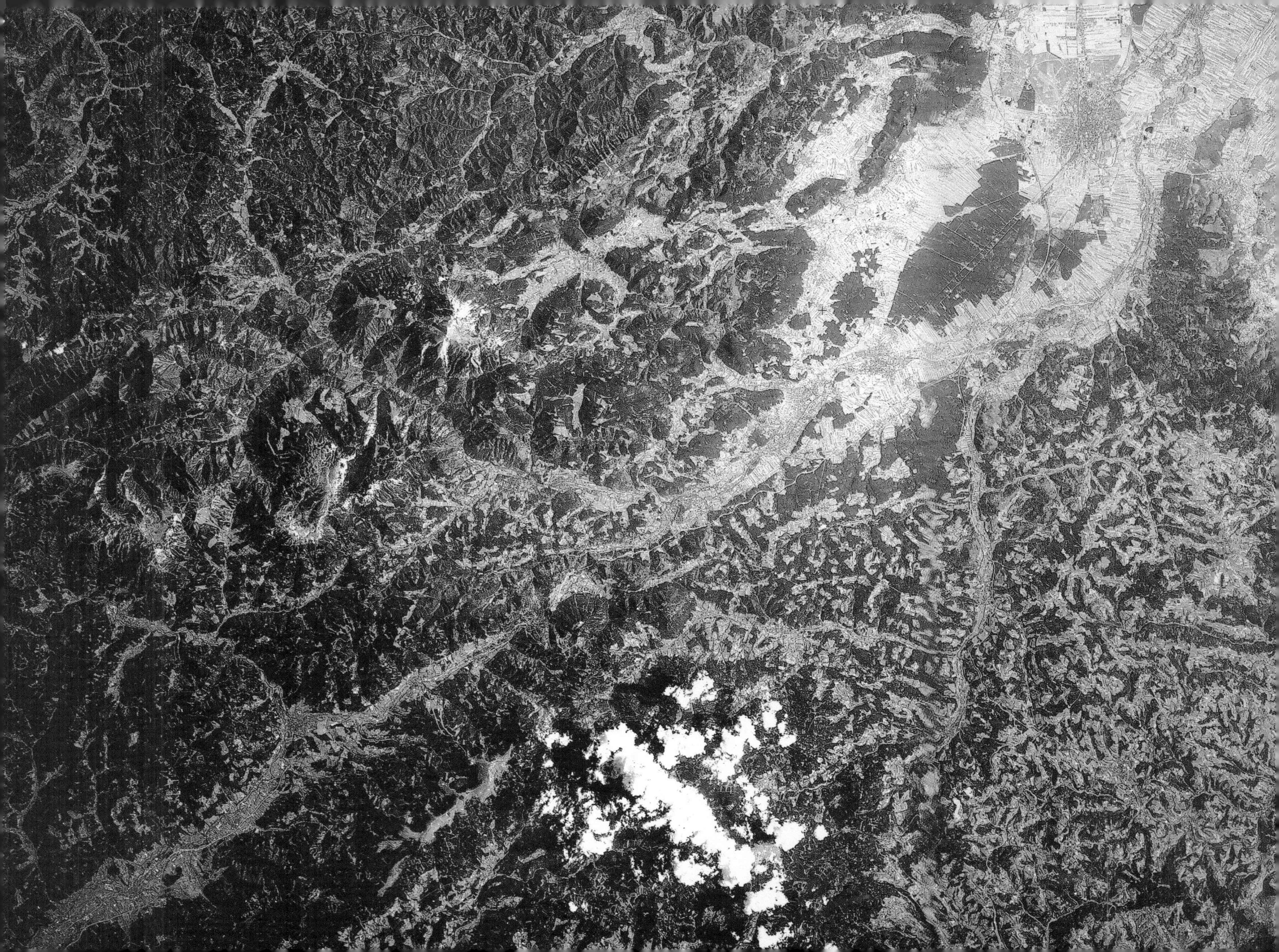

Franz Zwickl · Wolfgang Hartl

Die Sonnenwelt der Zauberberge

The Golden World of Magical Mountains

edition gutenberg

Texte: Christa Bergwald, Wolfgang Hartl, Franz Zwickl, Robert Pap und Georg Bauernfeind

Coverbild und Fotos*, Reproarbeit: Franz Zwickl
mit Dank an Helga für die Unterstützung bei der Fotoarbeit
Grafik, Ausführung: ArtGraphic – Wolfgang Hartl, Marlies Kirchler
Texte: Christa Bergwald, Wolfgang Hartl, Franz Zwickl,
Georg Bauernfeind und Robert Pap
Übersetzung: Michael Schagerl
Lektorat: Johannes Waldherr, Andrew Smith
Druck: Grasl Druck & Neue Medien

*Weltatlas S. 1 von Geoatlas, Satellitenbild S. 2 mit freundlicher
Zustimmung der Tourismusregion Niederösterreich Süd alpin,
Portraits Umschlag: Foto Irene

„Die Sonnenwelt der Zauberberge"

2003 Franz Zwickl und Wolfgang Hartl
ISBN 3-900323-60-7

Cover photograph and photos, reprographics: Franz Zwickl*
Many thanks to Helga for her support during the photo shoots
Graphics, realisation: ArtGraphic – Wolfgang Hartl, Marlies Kirchler
Texts: Christa Bergwald, Wolfgang Hartl, Franz Zwickl,
Georg Bauernfeind and Robert Pap
Translation: Michael Schagerl
Proofreading: Johannes Waldherr, Andrew Smith
Printed by Grasl Druck & Neue Medien

**Worldmap p. 1 von Geoatlas, satellite photo p. 2 kindly*
approved by the Tourism Region Alpine Lower Austria South,
portraits cover: Foto Irene

"The Golden World of Magical Mountains"

2003 Franz Zwickl and Wolfgang Hartl
ISBN 3-900323-60-7

Titelbild: Sonnenuntergang in der Wunderwelt der Zauberberge | *Title page: sunset in the Miraculous World of Magical Mountains*

Inhalt

Contents

in diesem reichen augenblick
da spüre ich das leben
berge von der frischen quelle
was hervorbricht aus der erde
atme ein bei jedem schritt
großen geist hab kraft zu geben
wahr ist dass ich hier
heute bin und wirklich werde

at this rich moment
I feel life
mountains of the fresh spring
breaking out of the earth
breathing in with every step
great spirit, got power to give
it's true that i am here
today and truly live

Wolfgang Hartl

Neue Welt

A New World

Ein großes Meer hat einst die Gegend hier bedeckt. Es wurde mit Schiffen befahren, so erzählt man. In den Nebel- und Wolkenseen verschwinden Dörfer und Felder – Erinnerungen an Zeiten, als am Ende des Erdmittelalters langsam die Entstehung unserer Alpen begann. Über Jahrmillionen wurden durch Einengungen, Verfaltungen und Überschiebungen Berge gebildet, zogen Wind und Wetter, Frost und Hitze, Eiszeiten und Tropenklima über das Land. Und noch vor 25 Millionen Jahren, als die Kalkfelsen von Schneeberg, Rax und Hoher Wand endgültig gehoben wurden, war hier Küstenlandschaft. Vulkane machten die Gegend unsicher. Palmen- und Zypressenhaine wuchsen im tropischen Monsunklima, Korallenriffe siedelten im warmen Wasser, urzeitliche Tiere lebten an den Stränden – lange bevor der Mensch die Landschaft betrat …

Once this area was covered by a great wide ocean with ships sailing on it, so the stories go. The villages and fields disappear in oceans of mist and clouds – reminiscent of the end of the Mesozoic era when the Alps gradually began to be formed. The mountains were formed over the course of millions of years by constriction, folding and overthrusting, and the land was exposed to wind and weather, frost and heat, ice ages and tropical climates. This was a coastal landscape 25 million years ago when the limestone crags of Schneeberg, Rax and Hoher Wand were finally raised up. Volcanic activity threatened the entire area. Vast areas of palm and cypress trees flourished in the tropical monsoon climate, underwater reefs were inhabited by colonies of coral, prehistoric life forms appeared on the beaches – long before man entered the scene …

Blick von der Weinzettlwand in den Adlitzgraben und Hippuritenriff bei Grünbach
View from Weinzettlwand towards Adlitzgraben and the lime reef near Grünbach
Seite 10/11: Blick von der Schneealpe Richtung Heukuppe | *Page 10/11: view from Schneealpe towards Heukuppe*

Aus dem Meer

F r o m   t h e   S e a

Versteinerte Kugelschnecken, Muscheln und andere Meerestiere aus dem Erdmittelalter wurden gefunden. Bis zu 120 Millionen Jahre alt sind die Versteinerungen, die man in der Gegend von Grünbach entdeckt hat. Reste von Palmen, Zypressen und Skelettfragmente fügen sich zu einem Puzzle zusammen, in dem die vergangene Meeres- und Küstenwelt der Region lebendig wird.

Petrified snails, shells and various other forms of sea life dating back to the Mesozoic Era were discovered. A geological find dates back approximately 120 million years – a petrified shell, found in the area around Grünbach. Fragments of palm trees, cypress and bone are all pieces of a puzzle that brings the ancient maritime and coastal flora and fauna back to life.

Oberer Adlitzgraben und versteinerte Herzmuschel bei Puchberg am Schneeberg | *Upper Adlitzgraben and petrified heart-shaped shell near Puchberg am Schneeberg*

Wasser ist Leben
Water is Life

Wasser ist die reine und klare Kraft aus den Bergen. Den Schatz, den sie in ihrem Inneren speichern, hüten und dann freigeben, findet man in stillen Quellen und rauschenden Bächen – Frische und Ursprung in diesem alten, lebendigen Land.
Wasser ist schier unerschöpflich und für alle da. Es bringt die Natur zum Blühen, es erfrischt und reinigt und es ist Lebensgrundlage für Menschen und Tiere.

Water is the pure and pristine power from the mountains. This treasure, which is stored, conserved and finally released, appears in many forms: tranquil springs and rushing creeks – freshness and origin in this ancient yet vibrant country.
Water seems to be inexhaustible and ever-present for everyone. It triggers nature's blossoming, it refreshes and cleanses, and it is the source of human and animal life.

Seite 14 bis 18: Schwarzazuflüsse; oben: junger Steinadler im Horst im Höllental
Pages 14 to 18: tributary creeks of the Schwarza River; above: golden eagle offspring in its nest in Höllental

Schwarzafluss und Wasseramsel | *Schwarza River and dipper*

Unzählige Quellen
Countless springs

… im Schneeberg- und Raxgebiet waren für die Bewohner von jeher Gegenstand von Sagen und Geschichten.
Unterirdische Klüfte, Seen, Grotten und Flüsse stellten in ihren Fantasien die Erklärung für die nie versiegenden Bäche dar. Embel und Schultes erzählen in ihren Reiseberichten um 1800 von einem großen unterirdischen See im Inneren des Schneeberges.
Bewiesen ist jedenfalls, dass Rax und Schneeberg mit ihren zahllosen Hohlräumen riesige Wasserspeicher sind und allein über die 1. Wiener Hochquellwasserleitung bis zu 200.000 m^3 Wasser pro Tag freigeben.

… used to provide the material for numerous tales and anecdotes typical of the region of the Schneeberg and Rax mountains. Subterraneous chasms, lakes, caves and mighty rivers inspired the local population's imagination to explain creeks that never run dry. In their travel notes from around 1800, Embel and Schultes mention a great subterranean lake inside Schneeberg. We know for a fact that the numerous karst caves in Rax and Schneeberg function as gigantic water reservoirs; the flow through the first Viennese water pipeline is estimated at a maximum of 200,000 m^3 *per day.*

Seite 22/23: Libelle | *Page 22/23: dragonfly*

Leberblümchen und Flusskrebs | *Liverwort and freshwater shrimp*

40 Jahre im Berg

Stored in the mountain for 40 years

Das Wasser war den Menschen hier von jeher kostbar und wird auch heute im Natur- und Wasserschutzgebiet der gesamten Rax-, Schneeberg- und Schneealpenregion geschützt.
Wie ein Schwamm hält der Berg bis zu 40 Jahre das kostbare Nass, das Regen und Schnee, gefiltert durch eine Humusschicht, in das Höhlenlabyrinth der Berge einspeisen.
Die intakte Bergwelt ist der Speicher für unsere Zukunft.

For the people living here, water has always been an invaluable treasure, and it still is today – the entire region of the Rax, Schneeberg and Schneealpe mountains is a protected nature and water reserve.
Just like a sponge, the mountain retains the precious liquid for up to 40 years in its interior; rain and snow feed the sponge, and cleansing topsoil filters the liquid on its way into the cave system.
An intact alpine world is our future reservoir.

Wasserreiter in Kaiserbrunn und die Wiener Hofburg | *Water carriers in Kaiserbrunn, and Vienna's imperial palace*

Kaiserwasser

Regent's Water

Das Wildwasser der Schwarza, so glaubte man noch vor 200 Jahren, käme direkt aus der Hölle – dem „Höllen"tal mit seinen himmelhohen Felswänden, Urwaldriesen, Sturzblöcken und seinen vielen Quellen.
Eine dieser Quellen ist in Kaiserbrunn gefasst, Kaiser Karl VI. entdeckte sie 1732 auf einem Jagdausflug. Sein Leibarzt stellte fest, dass dies das beste Wasser wäre, das er je getrunken habe – ein wahres Verjüngungsmittel. Auf schmalen Saumwegen brachten fortan kaiserliche „Wasserreiter" das begehrte Nass in zwei bis drei Tage dauernden Ritten an den kaiserlichen Hof nach Wien. 1865 schenkte Kaiser Franz Joseph I. die Kaiserbrunn-Quelle der Stadt Wien.

Two hundred years ago people used to believe that the mountain torrents of the Schwarza originated in hell and burst to daylight in the Valley of Hell (Höllental), with its sheer cliff faces, gigantic tree trunks, massive boulders and countless springs.
One of those springs has been routed to a well in Kaiserbrunn; Regent Karl VI discovered the spring in 1732 during a hunting trip. His personal doctor asserted that it was the best water ever consumed – a pure, rejuvenating liquid. From then on, royal "water riders" transported that precious liquid along narrow cut trails in two or three-day trips to the imperial court in Vienna. In 1865 the monarch Franz Joseph I gave the city of Vienna the Kaiserbrunn Spring as a gift.

Der Rohstoff des 3. Jahrtausends

The Raw Materials of the 3rd Millennium

„Keine Großstadt der Erde wird nach Vollendung dieses Riesenwerkes so treffliches Trinkwasser besitzen, wie Wien."
(F. Weidmann 1871, S. 112)
Wenn man bedenkt, wie mangelhaft die Wasserversorgung Wiens bis dahin war, kann man die Begeisterung Weidmanns nachvollziehen. Immer wieder traten wegen des schlechten Trinkwassers Typhus und Cholera auf. Lange Zeit gab es Probleme mit der Realisierung der Hochquellenwasserleitung, vielen war das Projekt zu teuer und sie plädierten für eine Leitung, die das Wasser von der Donau entnehmen sollte. 6.000 Arbeiter machten in 3,5 Jahren Bauzeit die Wasserleitung von Kaiserbrunn nach Wien schließlich wahr – 90 km lang, mit Quellfassungen, Speichern, gewaltigen Aquädukten, Rohrleitungen und Stollen wurde sie 1873 eröffnet. Tatsächlich hat kaum eine andere internationale Metropole heute so gutes Wasser wie Wien.

"Besides Vienna, no other city in the world will – after completion of this gigantic project – call such excellent drinking water its own" (F. Weidmann 1871, p. 112)
Considering the poor state of water distribution in the city of Vienna prior to the pipeline project, one can fully comprehend Weidmann's excitement. Due to the terrible quality of drinking water, typhoid and cholera used to be a major threat to the Viennese population. For a long time, realization of the pipeline project seemed rather problematic; the enormous costs proved to be the main argument against the project – a pipeline feeding water from the Danube to the city was many people's preferred choice. A workforce of 6,000 eventually completed the water pipeline from Kaiserbrunn to the city of Vienna in 3.5 years. Spanning a distance of 90 km, with wells, reservoirs, breathtaking aqueducts, pipes and shafts, it was officially opened in 1873. As a matter of fact, hardly any other international metropolis can boast such excellent water quality.

Kaiserbrunnen und Turmstein im Höllental | *Kaiserbrunn and Turmstein in Höllental*

„… die geheimnisvolle Quelle im Schneeberg, wo aus unbekannten Tiefen der Kaiserbrunnen ein dunkles kleines Bassin in einer kalten Felsengrotte füllte. Eine Blechkanne an langem Holzstiel wurde in die dunkle Kälte hinabgetaucht, und dann tranken wir das Wasser, das ganz anders schmeckte wie alles andere Wasser, man könnte sagen, säuerlicher. Und dieses märchenhafte Wasser … rinnt uns nun von selbst in die Häuser der Großstadt." (P. Altenberg 1918, S. 99 f)

"… the mysterious spring in Schneeberg, where, from unfathomed depths, the Kaiserbrunnen fills a small dark basin in a grotto. A metal tin attached to a long pole was poked deep down into the pitch black cold, and then we drank the water tasting so completely different from any other water, you could say it had a rather sour taste. And this magical water … now flows through our city taps."
(P. Altenberg 1918, p. 99)

Reservoir und Quellgrotte im Kaiserbrunnen | *Reservoir and spring grotto in Kaiserbrunnen*

Das Höllental war bis ins späte 18. Jahrhundert eine unzugängliche Wildnis. „Mit jedem Schritte vorwärts wurde die Gegend einsamer und unholder ... Die Gebirge wuchsen immer höher, ungeheure Felsenmassen thürmten sich zu einer fürchterlichen Höhe auf ... in schwindelnder Tiefe wühlte sich die Schwarza zwischen niedergestürzten Steinmassen schäumend und brausend hindurch ... Bald führte mich der Weg durch finstere, grauenvoll einsame Wälder, bald über äußerst kühne, über schreckbare Tiefen gespannte Brücken ... bald wieder aufwärts wo der Weg entweder blos in den Felsen gearbeitet war, oder wohl gar theilweise, gleich einem hölzernen Gange, auf unten an die Felsen gestemmten Baumstämmen ruhte ..." (F. X. Embel 1803, S. 129 ff)
Jetzt führen eine bequeme Straße und der Wasserleitungsweg durch das Höllental. Reste dieser einstigen Urlandschaft sind aber bis heute erhalten geblieben.

Until the late 18th century, Höllental was an inaccessible wilderness. "With each step forward the area grew lonelier and more inhospitable ... The mountains constantly grew taller, immense rock massifs towered to frightening heights ... and deep down below, the Schwarza River carved out its course in furious and foaming ways through the fallen boulders ... The trail led through dark and desperately lonesome woods, and soon afterwards across a treacherous abyss spanned by a breathtaking, rickety bridge ... Soon the trail ascended on poorly secured rocky terrain or along a wooden walkway resting on beams worked into the rock ..." (F. X. Embel 1803, p. 129)
Today, Höllental has been made accessible by a winding road and the trail that runs parallel to the water pipeline, although much still remains of the former rough territory.

Wasserleitungsweg im Höllental | *Waterside trail*

Seite 34 bis 39: Flussansichten der Schwarza | *Pp. 34 to 39: riverside impressions of the Schwarza*

Wie ein smaragdgrünes Band

Like an emerald ribbon

„… (zieht) die Schwarza ihre herrlichen grünen Wellen, oft aufbrausend über die mächtigen Steinblöcke in ihrem Bette, dann wieder über die dunkle Tiefe in stillem, leisem Zuge hinübergleitend, von der eilenden Forelle scharenweise durchzogen …" (A. Schmidl 1831, S. 251 f)

"… the Schwarza River flows in beautiful and lush green waves, sometimes rapidly shooting over mighty boulders in its way, sometimes quietly gliding across the dark depths, inhabited by droves of darting trout …" (A. Schmidl 1831, p. 251)

Donau in Budapest | *The Danube at Budapest*

Schwarzes Tal — schwarzes Meer

Black valley – Black Sea

Wasser hat vielen Orten und Gebieten ihren Namen gegeben: Gloggnitz (slaw. „glucksender Bach"), Würflach (12. Jhdt. „Wirbelache"), Stuppach (12. Jhdt. „stäubender Bach"), Naßwald, Naßalm, Rohr (15. Jhdt. „Sumpf", „Röhricht"), Krumbach, Feistritz (slaw. „Wildbach") etc.
Dieses Wasser läuft über Kieselsteine und Sandkörner, es ist in beständigem Fließen in Bächen, Flüssen und Strömen, die sich alle in der Donau und irgendwann im Meer sammeln – im Schwarzen Meer, dessen Name sich allerdings nicht wirklich von der Schwarza und dem Schwarzatal ableitet.

Water gave its name to a great many villages and regions: Gloggnitz (Slavic "gurgling creek"), Würflach (12th cent. "swirling brook"), Stuppach (12th cent. "foaming creek"), Nasswald, Nassalm, Rohr (15th cent. "swamp", "reed"), Krumbach, Feistritz (Slavic "whitewater") etc.
Flowing over pebbles and fine grains of sand, it is in constant motion in creeks, in streams and in mighty rivers, which all flow into the Danube and finally make their way to the Black Sea, the name of which is not in fact derived from the Schwarza or the Schwarza Valley.

Alles Wälder

Woods Everywhere

Der Wald ist mehr als eine Ansammlung von Bäumen – ein sensibles Ökosystem, Lebensraum für Pflanzen und Tiere, Reservoir für klare Luft, Erholungsraum für den Menschen.
Wem der Wald fremd ist, dem können die Laute und Geräusche fast erschreckend klingen. Sie werden laut, dann verebben sie wieder.
Nur der Stille findet ihn, den Wald – sonst flieht er und nur die Bäume bleiben übrig. Manch einer sieht dann den Wald vor lauter Bäumen nicht mehr.

The forest is much more than a mere collection of trees – it is a highly sensitive ecosystem, an living space for plants and animals alike, an reservoir of pristine air, and a recreation area for humans. Anyone who is a stranger to the forest might be frightened by the sounds and the noises, which all grow loud and threatening and then fade away again.
The forest reveals itself only to the quiet beholder – to all other, it escapes, but for the trees. Quite a few cannot see the wood for the trees.

„Alles Walzer"

Seite 44 bis 47: Waldstimmungen im Semmeringgebiet | *Pp. 44 to 47: forest moods in the Semmering region*

Wildes Waldland war einst die ganze Region. Urwälder machten jeden Weg von einem Dorf zum anderen, jede Reise über den Wechsel oder den Semmering zum gefährlichen Abenteuer. Nur schmale Saumpfade führten durch die Gebirgswildnis, in der Bären, Wölfe, Auerochsen, Luchse und Räuber hausten. Da konnte es schon geschehen, dass den verängstigten Leuten Gespenster oder die Habergeiß begegneten, dass Hexen oder der Teufel die Wanderer begleiteten oder verfolgten, narrten, entführten und in Gefahr brachten. Und trotz aller Erschließung ist die Gegend in manchen Bereichen bis heute Urland geblieben, das sich den Menschen auf eigene Art entzieht.

The entire region once used to be gigantic inhospitable undergrowth and forest. Journeying through the wild and untamed forests from one village to another, travelling across the Semmering or the Wechsel passes proved tiring and hazardous adventures. Nothing more than narrow trails led through the eerie mountain wilderness, which was inhabited by wild creatures such as bears, wolves, aurochs, pumas and robbers. It could well happen that scared travellers were haunted by ghosts or Habergeiss, that witches or the devil himself accompanied and chased travellers, tricked them, abducted them and put them in danger. And despite all explorations, vast parts of the region have retained their original, untamed character, which in its own way is still alien to humans.

Lebens-Raum

Living Space

Da sind die hohen Fichtenwälder des Semmeringgebietes mit dunklen Stämmen. In ihrem Schatten liegt weicher Moosboden, der mit seinen unzähligen Ameisen, Käfern und Spinnen ein Wald im Kleinen ist. Da sind die Mischwälder der Buckligen Welt mit dichtem Gestrüpp von Erlenbüschen und Dornsträuchern, im Herbst ein leuchtendes Farbenspiel. Wie vielfältig sind die Wälder des Rax-Schneeberggebietes mit ihren Fichten, untermischt mit Rot- und Schwarzföhren, Buchen, Lärchen, Linden und Eichen, mit Pilzen und Heidelbeeren. Weiter oben stehen die Bäume nicht mehr so hoch, sie sind verknorrter und starrer durch den stürmenden Wetterwind. Auf den Höhen wachsen nur mehr einzelne Föhren und Latschengestrüpp.

The dark, immovable trunks of fir trees stand tall and strong in the Semmering area. Far below, in the cooling shade of the firs, spongy and cool moss covers the ground, inhabited by countless ants, beetles and spiders – a miniature forest in its own right. The mixed forests of Bucklige Welt are characterized by thorny, dense brush; in autumn it changes into a playground of bright and shiny colours. The forests of the Rax-Schneeberg region boast enormous diversity, with fir trees, spruces, beeches, larches, limes and oak trees, fungi and blackberries. Higher up the trees do not stand as tall any more, they are exposed and thus shaped and moulded by the fierce forces of the weather. It is but a few single firs and low-lying brush weathering the forces of nature up on the heights.

Bergwald und Eichhörnchen am Stammbaum | *Mountain forest and squirrel on its tree*

Dahoam is dahoam – im Wühlmausnest und hohen Gras | *Home sweet home – in the vole's nest and the high grass*

Optisch festgehaltene Akustik: Grillengezirpe erzeugt auch Luftschwingungen, nicht nur schlaflose Nächte ...

Sound caught on camera: the chirping of the cricket not only produces airwaves but also causes sleepless nights ...

Drei kleine Sensationen:
1. Die Holzschlupfwespe spürt nach Gehör einen bis zu 4 cm tief im Holz liegenden Schädling auf, bohrt mit ihrer Legröhre durch das Holz, sticht in die Raupe und nutzt sie als Puppenwiege.
2. Durch die Nachzucht wird der Schädling vernichtet – und eine neue Holzschlupfwespe entsteht.
3. Dieses Foto.

Three small marvels:
1. The ichneumon fly senses a hidden parasite (up to 4 cm away), drills through the wood, pierces the larva and uses it as a cradle.
2. The parasite is killed off by this breeding process and eventually a young ichneumon fly emerges.
3. This photograph.

Ein Weberknecht zieht sich um – eine Spinne ist ausgezogen. | *The change of attire of a daddy longlegs – a spider has moved out.*

Baumwunder

Zufall trägt den Samen hin – der Baum kann sich seinen Platz nicht aussuchen, er muss ihn erst „erobern" in Sturm und Wetter. Da wächst er langsam, biegt sich fügsam um Hindernisse herum, um nicht geknickt zu werden, hat Sonne und Regen, gute und schlechte Jahre. Er ist beharrlich. Äste brechen ab, die Rinde wird beschädigt, er wächst weiter und wird alt, wenn man ihn lässt. Die Kraft nimmt er aus den tiefen Wurzeln.
Im Winter, wenn der Baum kahl ist, kann man sein Wesen besser erkennen. Da ist ein trauriger Baum; einer, der seine Äste wie Arme ausstreckt; ein anderer, kleiner und frecher; und ein solcher, der nichts als groß und einsam ist.
Er ist kein Wunderbaum, sondern ein gewöhnlicher – und dennoch ein Baumwunder: früher von den Menschen verehrt, der erste Tempel, in dem der Geist einer Gottheit hauste; das Symbol der Weltachse, welche Unterwelt, Erde und Himmel miteinander verband; das Sinnbild ewigen Lebens.
Heute ist er ein Zeichen für Wachstum und gesünderes Leben. Wir schauen zu ihm auf, kennen ihn als Nistbaum von Vögeln, als Kletter- und Obstbaum. Wir scheuen uns, einen Baum zu fällen; bauen Straßen und Wege dicht um ihn herum, lassen ihn auf Inseln im Verkehr stehen. Einen Baum pflanzen oder einen Baum fällen kann heute zum Politikum werden.

Tausendjährige Eiche bei Aspang | *Thousand-year-old oak near Aspang*

Miracle trees

By pure chance is the seed carried and dropped – it is not the tree's will to select its living space, it must be fought for and "captured" in fierce storms and inclement weather. Then the tree grows slowly skywards, willingly winding around obstacles, always careful not to get bent, it experiences rain and shine, good and bad years. It is persistent. Branches are ripped off, bark is damaged, it continues to grow higher and older, if its environment allows. Its firmly planted root system is the driving force behind its constant growth.
The tree's true identity can easily be discovered in the wintertime when it is stripped bare of its protective foliage. Here, the sad sight of a tree stretching out its branches like arms; there, a short and stout one; and another that seems just tall and lonely.
It is not a miracle tree, just a normal one – yet still a miracle in wood: worshipped by humans in olden days, the first temple inhabited by the spirit of a god; the symbol of the axis of the world connecting underworld, earth and sky, the symbol of eternal life. Today it has become synonymous with growth and a healthier life(style). We look up to it, we know it as the place where birds nest, as a natural climbing frame and as the fruit-bearing part of an orchard. We shy away from felling a tree; we build our roads and trails around it, we let it stay on restricted patches of soil surrounded by the roaring tarmac of stop-and-go. To plant or to fell might be a political issue nowadays.

Der „Vier-Brüder-Baum" wächst bei Prigglitz. Vor tausend Jahren hat das Wild die kleine Schwarzkiefer verbissen. Als wollte der Baum seine Lebenskraft gerade deshalb beweisen, sind ihm statt einem gar vier Triebe gewachsen. Die Natur hat ihm weiter zugesetzt – Blitzschlag und Absprengungen haben ihm nur zwei Triebe gelassen, dem tausend Jahre alten Baum.
Der „Sesserlbaum" steht in der Nähe von Ternitz – irgendjemand hat im Laufe der Jahre seine Äste immer wieder entlang eines Zaunes niedergebunden. Von da aus sind seine Triebe kerzengerade zum Licht hinaufgewachsen. Den Zaun gibt es heute nicht mehr, nur mehr die waagrechten Äste und die aufrecht in die Höhe stehenden Triebe. Der Baum hat sich angepasst, in den vielen Jahren aber auch beharrlich das Beste aus seiner Situation gemacht und sich geholt, was er brauchte.

The "Four Brothers Tree" grows near Prigglitz. A thousand years ago, wild animals did lasting damage to the tender buds of the Austrian pine. As if the tree has every intention of proving its will to live nonetheless, it grew four trunks rather than one. Nature further challenged the thousand-year-old tree by striking it with lightning, leaving it only two trunks.
The "Chair Tree" grows near Ternitz – over the years, somebody kept tying the tree's branches to a fence. Tying it down could not prevent the branches from growing straight towards the light. The fence no longer exists today, but the horizontal and vertical branches still do. The tree has adapted to its unnatural situation and has never ceased to get everything it needed to carry on living.

Edelkastanie in Buchbach | *Chestnut in Buchbach*

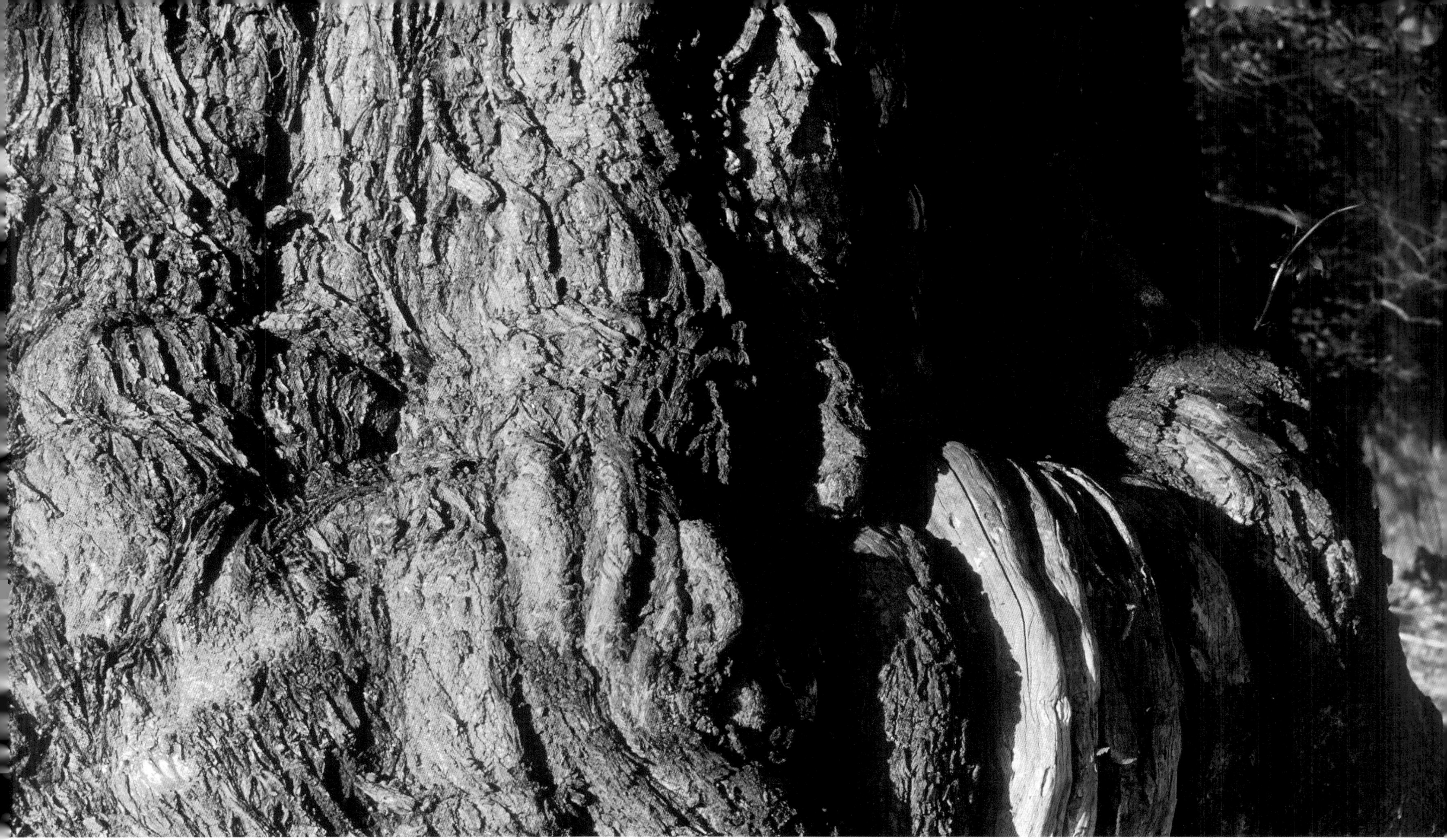

Außergewöhnliche Äste laden seltene Gäste: Lindenbaummonster in Friedersdorf und Uhu.
Extravagant branches invite rare guests: the Lime Tree Monster in Friedersdorf and an eagle owl

Es gibt sie

They do exist

… Orte der Stille und des Friedens, wo wir uns wohlfühlen, wo wir bleiben können – verborgene gute Plätze. Die Menschen früher haben sie gekannt und genutzt – Wiesen, Quellen, Steine, Bäume, Berghöhlen, Waldlichtungen. Viele christliche Kirchen befinden sich heute an Stellen alter, heidnischer Kultstätten.
Das „Geiskircherl", eine Durchgangshöhle, liegt oberhalb des Adlitzgrabens, ein schlichter Felsenraum mit einem Tisch und zwei Bänken. Vielleicht ist es eine uralte heidnische Kultstätte (keltisch „geis" bedeutet „heilig"). Seit 1913 befindet sich hier eine Marienandacht, vom christlichen Verband der weiblichen Hausbediensteten gestiftet.
Wenn wir aufbrechen, werden wir ihn entdecken – jeder von uns „seinen" eigenen Platz.

… those places of tranquillity and peace where we feel at ease and where we can stay – well hidden, good places; all we need is to head for them. In earlier days, people used to know and frequent such places – meadows, springs, rocks, trees, caves, clearings in the deep dark forest. Many Christian churches have been erected on the old, heathen sites of worship.
"Geiskircherl", a walk-through cave, is located high above Adlitzgraben. Maybe it is an ancient heathen place of importance (Celtic "geis" means "sacred"). Ever since 1913, a plain carved out area with a table and two pews has served as a place where the Virgin Mary can be worshipped – founded by the Christian Union of female household staff.
If we only take the time, we will discover it – every one of us has our very own personal place.

Geiskircherl oberhalb des Adlitzgrabens und frühchristliche Kultstätte in Mariensee
Geiskircherl above Adlitzgraben and an early Christian place of worship in Mariensee

Hohler Stein bei Witzelsberg und Steinkreis bei Krumbach | *Hollowed boulder near Witzelsberg and stone circle near Krumbach*

Heilige & Teufel
Saints & Devils

… haben die Gegend hier nicht spurlos verlassen, ihre Abdrücke sind geblieben. Steine mit Vertiefungen, Grübchen und Schalen gibt es überall – man ist versucht, sie für etwas Besonderes zu halten, sie mit Legenden und Sagen in Verbindung zu bringen. Von solchen Plätzen erhoffte man sich wunderbare Heilung und die Erfüllung besonderer Wünsche.
Das archäologische Rätselraten um die Entstehung solcher Schalensteine, die man in allen Erdteilen findet, ist noch im Gange. Ob die Vertiefungen, in denen sich seltsamerweise auch in längeren Trockenperioden Wasser hält, durch Erosionen, organische Säuren oder durch Baumwurzeln entstanden oder von Menschenhand gemacht worden sind, ob sie heidnische Kultplätze oder christliche Taufsteine waren, weiß niemand.

… have not left the area around here untouched, and the marks they left have remained to this day. Indented rocks, rock basins are ubiquitous around here – one is tempted to associate these features with the supernatural, to consider them something special and to attribute them to legends and fanciful tales. It was these sites that led people to hope for healing miracles and the fulfilment of their innermost wishes. Archaeology still has not been able to put a finger on the precise evolution of these rock basins, which can be found on all continents. Whether it was erosion, organic acids or massive roots deforming the rock, which stores water through prolonged dry periods as if by magic, or whether the rock was moulded by man to serve as a heathen worshipping site or Christian baptism stone, nobody can say for certain.

Verborgenes
Hidden Treasures

Die Gegend um Payerbach ist auch heute noch ein stilles Gebiet. Dort findet man an einer Stelle von Moos überzogene, aufrecht stehende Tragsteine, mit mächtigen Decksteinen abgedeckt; in die Steinplatte der Hinterwand waren Schalen eingearbeitet. Wahrscheinlich ist es ein megalithisches Bauwerk aus der Zeit um oder vor 1000 v. Chr. – einer Zeit, in der die Menschen hier schon begonnen haben, Erz abzubauen. Der Dolmen war vermutlich ein Kultplatz, ein Ort für Opferhandlungen und Weissagungen. Rund um den Dolmen ist ein Steinkreis zu erkennen, vor dem Eingang liegt ein umgestürzter Menhir mit eingemeißelten Ringen. Oft hat man Dolmen an „besonderen" Plätzen errichtet. Die Bodenstrahlung ist an diesem Ort besonders stark.

The region around Payerbach is still largely undisturbed. There you will find moss-covered stone pillars, standing upright and topped with huge pieces of rock; shells were embedded in the stone slab of the back wall. This is probably is a megalithic structure dating back to around 1000 B. C., when people in this region had already started mining ore. The dolmen was probably the site of cult activities, a place where sacrifices and prophecies were made. A circle of stones can be made out around the dolmen, in front of the entrance lies a toppled menhir with circles carved in to it. Dolmens were often set up in "special" places. The soil radiation at this site is particularly strong.

Insgesamt 40 Hügelgräber aus keltisch-römischer Zeit hat man in den Wäldern und auf den Feldern von Hochneukirchen gefunden – Brandgräber mit gemauerten Grabkammern und großen Erdhügeln. Die Verstorbenen wurden mit Kleidung, Schmuck und Speisenbeigaben auf Scheiterhaufen verbrannt und dann in Urnen in den Grabhügeln beigesetzt. „Schatzfunde" wie römische Münzen (ca. 260 n. Chr.), ein Haustorschlüssel, Grabsteine, Fibeln, Ton- und Geschirrscherben lassen die Zeit lebendig werden, in der Menschen entlang der „Hochneukirchnerstraße" siedelten. Als einer der römischen Verkehrswege führte sie von Erlach über Pitten, Krumbach und Hochneukirchen bis ins heutige Ungarn.

A total of 40 Celtic-Roman cairns (or tombs) were discovered in the forests and fields of Hochneukirchen – cremation tombs with a burial chamber made of brick and large mounds of earth. The deceased were placed on a pyre, fully dressed and bejewelled and equipped with food; they were then cremated and their ashes sealed in an urn and finally put to rest in the tomb. "Finds" such as Roman coins (approx. 260 A. D.), a door key, tombstones, brooches, shattered earthenware and crockery allow us to reconstruct and relive the era of the peoples who settled along the "Hochneukirchner Road". As one of the major Roman traffic routes, it connected Erlachus, Pitten, Krumbach and Hochneukirchen and crossed into present-day Hungary.

Dolmen bei Payerbach und Römergrab in Hochneukirchen | *Dolmen near Payerbach and Roman tomb in Hochneukirchen*

In der Osternacht werden die Osterfeuer angezündet. Die hellen Punkte leuchten dann auf den Hügeln und Bergen, über dem ganzen Tal liegt Brandgeruch. Wer über das Feuer springt, wird bald heiraten, sagt man. Als Kinder haben wir glühende Äste in die Luft geschmissen und den Funkenflug bestaunt.
Feuer zieht magisch an, es ist lebensnotwendig, es wärmt in der Kälte. Seit Urzeiten war es den Menschen und Göttern heilig, das Symbol für die strahlende, lebenspendende Sonne. Mit dem Osterfeuer wurde sie begrüßt, als Siegerin über den langen, kalten Winter.
Osternacht ist nach dem ersten Frühlingsvollmond. Das starke Licht, das zuvor vertrieben war, tritt jetzt wieder ein; das Dunkle ist draußen. Im Licht wachen die Farben auf. Die Zeit des Blühens, des Lebens beginnt.

Easter fires are lit on Easter night. Hills and mountains near and far are dotted with bright lights, the smell of fire wafts throughout the entire valley. It is believed that anyone who jumps across the fire will soon be married. When I was a child, we would grasp glowing branches, throw them into the air and get excited by the glowing sparks.
Fire has a magic attraction, it is essential to life, it keeps out the cold. Since mankind's earliest days, fire has been sacred to men and gods, it has been the radiant and life-giving symbol of the sun. The sun was welcomed back with Easter fires after the victorious defeat of long and cold winters.
Easter night falls after the first full moon of spring. The strong light, which was driven away during the winter, returns to rise in the sky; darkness is banished. Colours come back to life in the light. The season of blossoming, of life commences.

Osterfeuer in Kirchberg (Am Stein) und in Gloggnitz | *Easter fire in Kirchberg (Am Stein) and in Gloggnitz*

Panorama mit Burgruine Klamm und Adlitzgraben | *Panoramic view with the ruins of Klamm and Adlitzgraben*

Hinter den Mauern

Behind The Walls

Uralte Burgen liegen auf den Felsen und Hügeln der Region – man hat den Eindruck, sie bewachen die Täler heute so wie damals, als Reisende durch das Land zogen und den Burgherren für die Sicherung und Benützung der Wege Maut zahlten, als die Bauern aus den Tälern ihre Tribute ablieferten und in den Festungen Zuflucht und Verteidigung gegen Angriffe von außen fanden. Unnahbar stehen die Mauern, hinter denen Macht, Reichtum, Kultur und Fortschritt herrschten. Bis heute verbergen sie Geheimnisse, schweigend erzählen sie Geschichte und Geschichten vom vergangenen Leben und Treiben, von der Großzügigkeit, Tapferkeit und Grausamkeit ihrer Besitzer.

Ancient castles are perched high up on cliffs and hills in the region – one has the impression that they are guarding the valleys today, just as they used to in olden days, when travellers used to have to pay toll to the owner of the castle for travelling along safe paths, when farmers used to give parts of their harvest in exchange for protection from ferocious attacks. The walls stand invincible, sheltering wealth, power, culture and progress. To this day they hold their secrets and tales, a mute narration of history and stories of wheeling and dealing, of generosity, courage and cruelty alike of their owners.

Mit ihren Türmen, Pechnasen und Wehrgängen waren Festungen wie Kranichberg Pass- und Straßensperre, immer wieder Zufluchtsort vor drohenden Gefahren und verwaltungspolitische Zentren. Im Laufe der Jahrhunderte erlebte die Burg Höhen und Tiefen, Feste, Fehden und Kriege, Umbauten, Brände und wechselvolle Schicksale ihrer Besitzer. Die schauerliche „Eiserne Jungfrau" erinnert an dunkle Vergangenheit. In dieser aufklappbaren Hinrichtungsmaschine wurde das Opfer von eisernen Dornen durchbohrt, wenn man die „Jungfrau" schloss. Bis heute sind um die renovierte Festung mit ihrem mittelalterlichen Bergfried, der Burgkapelle aus dem 15. Jahrhundert und den Gewölben der über 300 Jahre alten ehemaligen Schlossbrauerei Geschichten lebendig.

With their turrets, pitch shoots and battlemented parapets, castles such as Kranichberg served as checkpoints along roads and mountain passes as well as strongholds and places of refuge when danger was imminent. They were also administrative centres. Conquered in 1486, this castle experienced many ups and downs, feasts, conflicts and wars, restructuring, fires and changing fates of its owners throughout the centuries. The brutal "Iron Maiden" is reminiscent of history's darker days. This killing machine could be opened and the victim squeezed inside; when the "Maiden" was closed, the iron spikes on the inside pierced the victim. Stories about the castle, with its chapel dating back to the 15th century and vaults of the 300-year-old brewery, are still told to this day.

Eiserne Jungfrau und Burgkapelle in der Burg Kranichberg | *Chapel and Iron Maiden in Castle Kranichberg*

In der Mitte des 12. Jahrhunderts erstmals urkundlich erwähnt, war die Burg Feistritz einst Talsperre und Sicherung gegen feindliche Einfälle vom Pittental her – eine Burg von vielen in einer ganzen Verteidigungskette des Grenzlandes gegen Osten hin. Von hier aus sicherte man die Wege, die aus dem Pittental über Kranichberg zum Semmering führten und überwachte mit Feuersignalen das Land über große Entfernungen. Immer wieder gab es erbitterte Kämpfe, doch weder Matthias Corvinus noch die Türken konnten die Festung einnehmen. Die Burg wurde im Laufe der Zeit zu einem Schloss ausgebaut und später auch durch ihre Waffensammlung berühmt. In ihr befanden sich die Rüstung des Ritters Götz von Berlichingen und eine „Eiserne Jungfrau". Diese großen Schätze gibt es heute hier nicht mehr, wohl aber verbergen sich auch heute noch Kostbarkeiten hinter den Mauern: der Hungerturm und das Verlies, der Rittersaal mit seinem schönen Kreuzgewölbe, die Holztäfelungen aus dem 15. und 16. Jahrhundert, der mit Arkaden geschmückte Renaissancehof und die Burgkapelle mit Glasmalereien von 1557. Heute – wie Schloss Kranichberg und andere Burgen auch – in Privatbesitz, ist das restaurierte Schloss ein Stück Vergangenheit, jedoch erfüllt mit neuer Kreativität und Lebendigkeit.

Feistritz Castle is first mentioned in the records in the mid 12th century. As part of the defence chain in the eastern borderlands, it blocked off the Feistritz valley from enemy attacks launched along Pitten valley. This was the centre of defence, offering safety along the roads running from Pitten valley via Kranichberg towards Semmering and watching over vast expanses of the countryside with fire signals. The area was constantly the site of fierce fighting, yet neither Matthias Corvinus nor the Turks could conquer the stronghold. The castle was gradually extended and underwent constant improvement; in later years, its collection of armour became famous far and near. The armoury of Götz von Berlichingen and an Iron Maiden were among its prize pieces. These treasures can no longer be viewed here, but the walls still house some gems, for instance the keep and the dungeon, the knights' hall with its perfect cross vaulting, the rich wood panelling from the 15th and 16th centuries, the Renaissance courtyard surrounded by cloisters, and the chapel with its stained-glass windows dating back to 1557. Like Kranichberg and other castles, Feistritz is privately owned and is a renovated testimony to history yet filled with creativity and new life.

Rittersaal und Bibliothek in der Burg Feistritz | *Knights' hall and library in Feistritz Castle*

Einstieg in unterirdische Fluchtwege | *Descent into escape paths*

Der Schatz im Berg

Mountain Treasure

Geschichten von Kostbarkeiten und wertvollen Gesteinen, sorgsam gehütet von Berggeistern und Zwergen, sind in der ganzen Region lebendig. Auf dem Silbersberg bei Prigglitz soll sogar ein Drache die Schätze im Innern des Bergwerks bewacht haben.

Manche dieser Reichtümer gaben die Berge frei: Kupfer an den Hängen von Rax und Schneeberg, Eisenerz am Grillenberg bei Payerbach, in Reichenau und bei Pitten, Schwerspat am Sonnwendstein und am Silbersberg, Braunkohle in Enzenreith, Steinkohle in Grünbach, Silber und Gold am Silbersberg (16. bis 19. Jhdt.) und in Trattenbach (ab 16. Jhdt.), Gips in Schottwien und Puchberg, Magnesit in Eichberg, Gloggnitz und Aue (19. und 20. Jhdt.) und Kupferkies bei Trattenbach.

Die Bergbaugeschichte der Region ist wahrlich uralt: Durch die dichten Urwälder des Schwarza- und Preintales drangen die Illyrer vor, um an den Hängen von Rax und Schneeberg nach Kupfer zu suchen, aus dem sie Werkzeuge, Waffen und Schmuckstücke herstellen konnten. In mühevoller Arbeit bauten sie von ca. 1100 bis 800 v. Chr. das Erz ab – zuerst im Tagbau (heute noch erinnern daran zahlreiche trichterförmige Vertiefungen im Gelände, die „Pingen"), dann schließlich tief im Berg. Im Höllental, am Grillenberg und bei Hirschwang wurden Hüttenplätze, ein Bronzemesser, eine Axt und ein Serpentinschwert aus dieser Zeit entdeckt.

Eisenerz baute man vom 17. Jahrhundert an bei Pitten ab und seit dem ausgehenden 18. Jahrhundert auch am Grillenberg bei Payerbach, bei Edlach und am Knappenberg. 350 m tief wurde es am Grillenberg bis Ende des 2. Weltkrieges aus dem Berg geholt, in Ternitz, aber auch sogar in Schlesien verhüttet und u. a. in den Eisen- und Hammerwerken von Hirschwang und

Glimmerschiefer, im Volksmund „Katzensilber"
Mica schist, formerly also called cat-silver

Edlach verarbeitet. Das Pittener Eisenwerk bezeichnete man im 19. Jahrhundert als das bedeutendste in Österreich unter der Enns. Die heute so idyllische, ruhige Landschaft war bis ins 20. Jahrhundert auch Industriegebiet. Für viele Bewohner hier bedeutete dies Arbeit und Wohlstand, für die Natur aber auch Eingriffe. So erforderte der enorme Holzbedarf für die Verhüttung der Erze die Schlägerung großer Waldgebiete.

Auch ein Gloggnitzer Hufschmied glaubte im 19. Jahrhundert an die Existenz eines Schatzes im Berg, als er große Braunkohlevorräte im Harter Berg bei Gloggnitz buchstäblich „roch". Tatsächlich wurde man fündig. Über 100 Jahre lang, bis 1949, baute man hier Braunkohle ab, bis zu 70.000 Tonnen jährlich. Die Grünbacher Steinkohle war im 19. und 20. Jahrhundert eine wichtige Stütze für die Rohstoffversorgung der Großstadt Wien. 1953/54 förderten hier über 1.000 Mann rund 600 Tonnen Kohle täglich und gruben bis zu 1.000 Meter unter Tag.

Als Kinder waren wir oft auf der Suche nach Schätzen im Berg. Alte Geschichten geisterten in unseren Köpfen herum und die Stollen eines aufgelassenen Bergwerks bei Prigglitz hatten eine magische Anziehungskraft. Im Eingangsbereich entdeckten wir schließlich, zwischen Steinen verborgen, eine „Silberader". Oft schlichen wir hin und fuhren vorsichtig mit den Fingern darüber, die dann ganz silbrig wurden. Die Tatsache, dass das „Silber" tatsächlich nur Katzensilber war, konnte meinen Traum vom Schatz im Berg nicht zerstören. Und viele Kostbarkeiten fand ich seither dort – wenn auch anderer Art, als ich als Kind geträumt hatte.

This region used to teem with ancient stories about treasure and valuable gemstones, carefully watched over and safeguarded by mountain spirits and dwarves. On Silbersberg near Prigglitz, a dragon was said to have guarded the hidden treasure inside the mines. Some of these treasures were made available to the people: the Rax and Schneeberg slopes were mined for copper, iron ore on Grillenberg near Payerbach, as well as in Reichenau and near Pitten, heavy spar on Sonnwendstein and Silbersberg, brown coal in Enzenreith, pit coal in Grünbach, silver and gold on Silbersberg (16th – 19th century) and in Trattenbach (16th century onwards), gypsum in Schottwien and Puchberg, magnesite in Eichberg, Gloggnitz and Aue (19th century) and copper pyrite near Trattenbach.

The history of mining in the region is truly long: the Illyrians came from the dense jungles of the Schwarza and Prein valleys to search the slopes of Rax and Schneeberg for copper to produce tools, weapons and ornaments. From approximately 1100 to 800 B. C., it was an excruciating mining process in open mines (today there are many funnel-shaped depressions in the terrain, so-called "glory holes"). Later on shafts were dug to mine the metal out of the rock. In Höllental, on Grillenberg and near Hirschwang, furnaces, a bronze knife, an axe and a serpentine sword were discovered, all of which back to that time.

Iron ore was mined near Pitten from the 17th century and from the end of the 18th century on Grillenberg near Payerbach, near Edlach and on Knappenberg. On Grillenberg the ore was brought up from as deep as 350m up until World War II, transported to the smelter mills in Ternitz or even in what is now the Czech Republic and processed in the iron works in Hirschwang and Edlach. In the 19th century, the iron mill in Pitten was said to be the most important mill south of the Enns River. What appears today to be an idyllic, tranquil region used to be heavily industrialized, until the 20th century. While many locals lived off and based their comfortable lifestyle on mining, the disadvantages to nature were plain to see. Extensive forest areas along the slopes of Rax and Schneeberg had to be deforested, because smelting iron ore required an enormous amount of energy.

A Gloggnitz blacksmith firmly believed there was treasure hidden in the mountain – when he literally "smelled" large reserves of brown coal in the 19th century. Brown coal was indeed found. For more than 100 years, until 1949, a total of 70,000 tons of brown coal a year was mined here. The discovery and mining of pit coal in Grünbach proved to be a vital source of energy for the capital of Vienna in the 19th and 20th century. In 1953/54 a workforce of more than 1,000 men mined around 600 tons of coal each day and dug down as deep as 1,000 metres below the surface.

When we were children, we would always be on the lookout for treasures in the mountain. Our heads were filled with the old tales, and the shafts of a closed mine near Prigglitz had a strong, magical attraction for us. In the area near the entrance to the mine, we discovered a silver vein, well hidden between rocks. We often secretly tiptoed there and gently brushed across it with our fingers, which consequently turned silvery. The fact that it was nothing more than fake silver (cat-silver) could not crush my dreams of treasure in the mountain. I have since found many a treasure there – though they have been of a different kind than I dreamed about as a child.

Auf den Wiesen

Across the Meadows

… kam mit der Dunkelheit kühle Luft aus dem Wald herüber. Kindertage auf dem Bauernhof. Das Geräusch der Melkmaschine im Stall bedeutete das Ende des Arbeitstages; es war die Zeit, wo wir im dämmrigen Licht des Waldes aus Reisig unser Lager bauten. In diesem kleinen Unterschlupf zu übernachten war unser großes Abenteuer. Einmal hat uns dabei der Dackel eines Försters aufgestöbert.

Der Wald war die weite Welt. Eine Wiener Familie, die bei uns zur Sommerfrische wohnte, nahm uns manchmal auf Ausflüge mit. So lernten wir Naßwald kennen, die Kientaler Hütte, die Rax. Rote Tupfer gehören auch ins Bild – Begonien auf den Fensterbrettern.

Die Welt ist seither für mich größer geworden. Auf meinen Reisen über Naßwald hinaus, an andere Orte der Welt, war das Heimweh nach den Bergen und dem Wald immer da. Ich bin zurückgekommen. Vieles hat sich hier verändert, manches ist gleich geblieben – das abendliche Geräusch der Melkmaschine, die Arbeiten im Stall. Aus der Abenddämmerung kommt wie ehedem die Stille, im Wald ist immer noch genug Platz, um Unterschlupfe zu bauen – hier in dieser (anderen) Welt.

Wer hier mit offenen Augen der Natur nachgeht, wird ein Kleinod nach dem anderen entdecken und wahr-nehmen. Das Licht ist heller, der Himmel klarer.

Hierher kann man wiederkommen, der Sehnsucht nach dem Geruch der Waldwiesen folgen, vor einem Baum stehen bleiben, auf den Almen des Wechsels Ausschau halten.

Die Landschaft dieser Region beginnt dort, wo das Steinfeld endet. In der Kleinräumigkeit hat sie ihre Vielfalt und ihre Eigenart erhalten – im pannonischen, mitteleuropäischen und alpinen Wald- und Bauernland mit einem Stück Hochgebirge. Jeder Berg, jeder Landstrich hat hier sein eigenes Gesicht.

Blick vom Kreuzberg auf Payerbach | *View from Kreuzberg to Payerbach*

… cool air wafted over from the woods as darkness fell. Childhood days on the farm. The monotonous sound of the milking machine announced the end of the working day; back in those days, in the fading twilight we would build our rickety shelters from dry fir tree branches. Spending the night in such a tiny makeshift shelter was our special adventure. Once we were discovered by a forester's dachshund.

For us, the forest was the big wide world. A Viennese family holidaying with us occasionally took us out on trips. This was how we came to know Nasswald, the Kientaler hut, and Rax. Red blotches were part of the image – begonias on windowsills.

Since then, the world has grown wider for me. A yearning for the familiar mountains and forests of home has always been present inside me on my journeys beyond Nasswald, taking me to other places on the globe. I have returned. A great many things have changed, some haven't – the milking machine's sound in the evening, the tasks in the cowshed. Dusk still releases tranquillity, the forest still offers plenty of space for creating shelters – it is all part of this (different) world, one hour's drive from Vienna: Anyone who looks for nature with their eyes wide open will discover one treasure after another. The light is brighter, the sky clearer.

This is a place to return to, longing for the scent of forest meadows, stopping in front of a tree, taking in the scenery from the Alpine pastures of Wechsel.

The landscape of this region begins where Steinfeld ends. Its particular nature and its diversity have been preserved in small areas – in the Pannonic, central European and Alpine forests and farmlands, with a high mountain area. Each mountain, each strip of land, possesses its very own characteristic features.

Seite 92/93: Sonnenuntergang hinter der Heukuppe | *Page 92/93: the sun sinks behind Heukuppe*

Die Berge rücken zusammen

The Mountains are moving in

… die mächtigen, wettergrauen Gebirgsstöcke von Rax und Schneeberg. Ruhig sind sie in den Höhen über dem Dunst der Niederungen. Selbst im Sommer ist dort noch Schnee zu finden. Zwischen den Felsen tun sich Täler mit Quellen und klaren Wasserläufen auf. Die hochgelegenen Almen auf dem Wechsel, die sich über den Höhenrücken dahinziehen, verwandeln sich im Sommer in blühende Paradiese – intakte Erholungsräume mit seltenen Pflanzen.

Wälder mit Baumriesen gibt es auf den sagenhaften Waldbergen von Semmering, Sonnwendstein und Otter – Berge mit einer Rundsicht bis weit in die Bucklige Welt hinein, deren graublaue Mugeln zum Horizont hin ineinander laufen.

… the mighty, weather-beaten mountain massifs of Rax and Schneeberg. Up on their slopes, perfect quiet dwells above the mist of the lowlands. Even in summer can you still find snow up there.

Rock gives way to ravines and valleys where springs and pristine streams run. In the summertime, the high pastures along the undulating crest of Wechsel are transformed into a blooming paradise – intact recreation areas boasting rare plant species.

Forests with gigantic trees can be found on the legendary Semmering, Sonnwendstein and Otter – mountains offering spectacular scenic vistas far into Bucklige Welt, whose blue-grey undulating countryside merges into the horizon.

Behutsamer Wind

Cautious Wind

... löst die Dunkelheit allmählich auf. In der Nacht ist viel Tau gefallen. Schnell trocknet die Wärme die Tropfen auf den Zweigen; wo im Dickicht oder auf Baumstöcken Spinnennetze gespannt sind, glitzern sie wie Silberfäden. Allmählich legt sich die Sonne auf die Wiesen, die nach Kräutern riechen und mit Käfern und Schmetterlingen bevölkert sind. Jetzt blüht auf dem Semmering und der Rams überall der Schwalbenwurzenzian und auf der Bodenwiese, der größten Alm des Schneeberggebietes, duften die Kohlröserl.
An heißen Tagen liegt der Himmel manchmal wie Dunkelheit über den Almen des Wechsels, klar und leer; es ist, als ob die Sonne zu klein werden würde für die Weite. Wechselvolles Spiel der Wolkentürme im August – man muss sie gesehen haben über den Hügeln der Buckligen Welt. Immer wieder formen sie sich neu, um über den Himmel zu wandern. In der Hitze bleibt es nur in den Wäldern kühl. Erst mit der Dämmerung kommt erfrischender Wind und alles atmet dann auf.
Auf dem Schneeberg und der Rax ist jetzt Frühling. Ganze Teppiche mit bunten Alpenblumen überziehen die Wiesen.
Bei warmem, regnerischem Wetter dampft der Wald, es riecht dann nach feuchter Erde, Pilzen, Moos und Erdbeeren. Man sagt, der Schneeberg zieht Unwetter an. Der Kaiserstein auf dem Gipfelplateau wurde im Lauf der Jahre etliche Male vom Blitzschlag zertrümmert. Nach solchen Gewittertagen stehen die Berge überklar, zum Greifen nah mit ihren goldgrünen Wiesen. Es ist so überaus einfach zu leben, hier in der Sonne.

... gradually disperses the darkness. The ground is heavy with dew. The warming rays of the sun dry up the last dewdrops on the twigs and branches; skilfully crafted spider webs in the undergrowth or spanning tree trunks glitter like silvery threads. Gradually the sun warms the meadows, which smell like hay and herbs and are populated by beetles and butterflies. Now the willow gentian is in full bloom up on Semmering and the Rams and across the largest Alpine pasture in the Schneeberg region, Bodenwiese, the scent of the moss cabbage-roses fills the air.
On hot days the sky sometimes feels clear and empty – almost like darkness cloaking the pastures of Wechsel, as if the sun might grow too small to shine across the vast countryside. August boasts a changeable rising and falling of towering clouds – one simply has to have experienced them rising over the undulating countryside in Bucklige Welt. They do not cease to reform and drift across the sky. Only the forests now offer cooling shelter from the beating heat. Only once the soothing wind sets in around dusk is there relief from the excessive heat.
Spring has arrived on Schneeberg and Rax. The alpine pastures are carpeted with colourful alpine flowers. The forest holds steaming moisture in warm rainy weather and the damp soil, mushrooms, moss and strawberries all radiate their pleasant aroma. It is believed that Schneeberg attracts thunderstorms. Over the years, the Kaiserstein, which rests on the plateau of the summit, has been smashed to pieces many a time by ferocious thunderstorms. The mountains stand strong and clear after such thunderstorms, so close that you might think you could reach out and grasp them with their gold and green meadows. Living here is so easy, living here in the sun.

Links: Heuschrecke, Seite 96/97: Mohnblumen | *Left: grasshopper, page 96/97: poppies*

Hinter einem Bauernhof bei Prigglitz liegt eine Waldwiese, rundherum stehen Fichten. Die Wiese ist zu klein, um gemäht zu werden. Weitläufig und abenteuerlich ist das Leben in diesem Gräserwald mit seinem grünen Blattgewirr, dem Thymian und Salbeikraut und den dichten Brennnesseln. Käfer sind unterwegs, klettern an den Halmen hinauf und schwirren in der Hitze über die Wiese. Da sind auch Schmetterlinge, blaue, rote und schwarze. Ruhe – und dennoch so viele Geräusche. Es ist ein Knistern, Rascheln und Summen zwischen den roten Disteln und Wiesenblumen, deren Farben sich im Gewirr mit vielerlei Grün vermischen.

Behind a remote farm near Prigglitz lies a forest clearing surrounded by firs. This meadow is too small to be mowed. Life is vast and filled with adventure in this grassy forest, in its maze of leaves, thyme and sage and dense patches of extra large nettles. It is a place teeming with life – beetles are on the move, climbing up leaves and buzz across the meadow in the heat. There are butterflies too – blue, red and black ones. Quiet – yet still such an abundance of noises. A crackling, rustling and humming goes on among the red thistles and flowers, whose colours perfectly blend in with the various shades of lush green.

Schwalbenschwanzraupe und -schmetterling | *A swallowtail caterpillar and butterfly*

Kaisermantel und Tagpfauenauge mit Gast auf einer Wiesenflockenblume | *Silver-washed fritillary, peacock butterfly and guest on meadow knapweed*

Türkenbundlilie und Orchidee auf der Gahnshauswiese | *Turk's cap lily, orchid in Gahnshaus meadow*

Landleben

Country Life

Es war ein verregneter Sommer in der Buckligen Welt. Die Wiesen konnten nicht gemäht werden und das Gras stand hoch – nichts als dürre Halme. Ich war irritiert. Wie sind wir doch gewohnt, dass unsere Landschaft gepflegt aussieht; wann machen wir uns schon Gedanken darüber, dass die Wiesen gemäht, die Sommerfelder das Jahr über bewirtschaftet werden müssen und dass trotz allen technischen Fortschritts diese Arbeit abhängig bleibt von Wind und Wetter. „Kaltenberg", „Holzschlag", „Wiesmath" – die Flur- und Ortsnamen sind Spuren aus einer Zeit, in der die Menschen begannen, das Berg- und Waldland urbar zu machen. Die Natur hat heute für die Bauern etwas von ihrem Schrecken verloren. Aber eine letzte, unwägbare Größe bleibt.

It was a rainy summer in Bucklige Welt. The meadows could not be mowed and the grass was standing tall – nothing but dry stems. I was irritated. We are all used to our countryside looking well cared for; do we ever think that meadows need mowing, the summer fields need work throughout the year, and despite all the technological progress agriculture still depends on the forces of wind and weather. "Kaltenberg" (cold mountain), "Holzschlag" (timber logging), "Wiesmath" (mowed meadow) – the names of fields and villages are reminders of a time when people started cultivating mountains and forests. Today, nature has lost some of its threat for the farmer. Yet one last unpredictable parameter remains.

Schloss und Ort Krumbach, Bucklige Welt | *The castle and village of Krumbach, Bucklige Welt*

Strohgedecktes Bauernhaus im Raum Hochneukirchen | *Thatched farmhouse in the vicinity of Hochneukirchen*

Zähigkeit, Optimismus und einiges Geschick gehören dazu, um als Landwirt durchzukommen. Gleichzeitig liegen hier aber große Chancen, das Gute am Althergebrachten und die vielseitigen Erfahrungen weiterzugeben und das Alte mit dem Neuen zu verbinden.

Perseverance, optimism and some skill are needed to survive as a farmer. Conversely, farmers have the great opportunity of passing on what is good in the old-fashioned traditions and of combining the old with the new.

Viele Bauern hier gehen einen guten Weg, finden tragbare und lebensfähige Kompromisse zwischen den Interessen marktorientierter Landwirtschaft und dem Schutz der Natur. Man sieht wieder mehr Schmetterlinge, Mohn- und Kornblumen auf den Feldern und mehr Insekten auf den Wiesen. Und so bleibt eine detailreiche, bewegte Vielfalt an Wiesen, Almen, Feldern, Wald und Bächen erhalten – Biotope mit großem Reichtum an Gräsern, Kräutern, Insekten und Kleintieren.

Many farmers around here take the middle road, find acceptable compromises between the market-oriented interests of agriculture and protecting the environment. More butterflies, poppy seed and cornflowers can be seen in the fields and more insects in the meadows. So there is still rich diversity in meadows, alpine pastures, fields, forest and creek – biotopes abundant in grasses, herbs, insects and small animals.

Sensenwetzen zu Hause in Prigglitz und Marienkäfer auf einer Gerstenähre | *Whetting a scythe at home in Prigglitz, ear of barley*

Marktnischen sind zu entdecken und zu nutzen. Biologische Lebensmittel in bester Qualität werden ab Hof verkauft und an den Gast gebracht. Denn auch die Gasthöfe und Hotels der Region verwenden zunehmend die gesunden Produkte der umliegenden Bauern.

Market niches must be found, developed and utilized. High quality organic, home-grown foods are sold to the customer directly from the farm. Also the inns and hotels of the region have also discovered the healthy produce grown by regional farmers and have added it to their menus.

Taubenkropfnelke | *Bladder campion*

Mit unseren vollen Terminkalendern sind wir Teile von Abläufen geworden, verlieren oft den Überblick über das Ganze. Mancher versäumt vielleicht Trends, bleibt aber weiter in große Zusammenhänge eingebunden – er weiß um das Werden, um Wachstum und Reife.
Man muss hier die richtigen Dinge zur richtigen Zeit tun, beobachten, dann handeln. Eine alte neue Form des (Über)Lebens – vielleicht ein anderes Maß für unsere Zeit der Hektik und Sachzwänge.

Driven by our busy schedules, we have become a part of a rat race, and all too often we lose sight of the bigger picture. Some may miss various trends, yet stay connected in the bigger picture – they know about being, growing and maturing.
One must do the right thing at the right time, look first, then act. An ancient formula for survival – perhaps it is a new standard for our hectic times and material pressures.

An den Sommermorgen habe ich als Kind immer die Kühe auf die taunasse Weide getrieben. Den Schimpfnamen „dumme Kuh" verstand ich schon damals nicht. Ich mag diese Tiere, sie strahlen Ruhe aus und stehen mit vier Beinen fest in ihrem Kuh-Leben. Ganz stolz war ich, wenn mir Zwölfjährigem die 25 riesigen Kühe brav auf dem 2 km langen Weg vom Stall zur Weide folgten. Erst später entdeckte ich, dass sie nicht mir, sondern der Leitkuh nachgetrottet waren.

On summer mornings, I would always drive the cows out into the dewy pasture. I have never understood the derogatory term "silly cow", for I like these animals. They radiate calmness and have their four legs firmly planted in their cow lives. As a twelve-year-old, I used to be so proud that 25 huge cows would follow me without much ado on our two kilometres from the shed to the pasture. It was only later that I discovered it wasn't me they were following, but their leading cow.

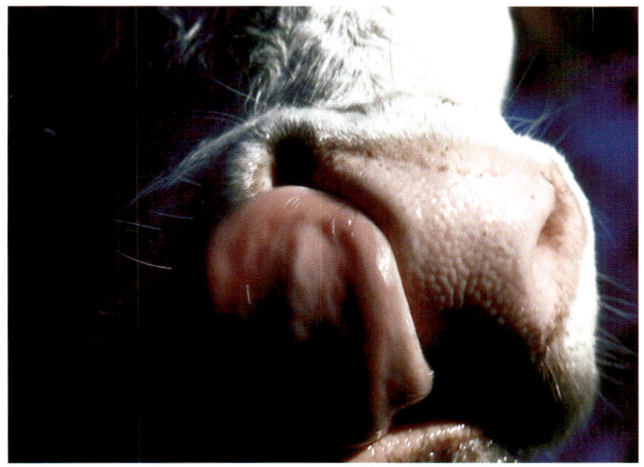

Die Almwirtschaft in den Ostalpen ist fast 4.000 Jahre alt. Und auch heute sind Almen unverzichtbar für die Erhaltung des ökologischen Gleichgewichts. Das Abweiden verhindert ein Zuwachsen der freien Flächen, hält Erosionen ab und mindert die Lawinengefahr. Ökologisch intakt, sind unsere Almen auch wertvoller Erholungsraum, Rückzugsgebiete für Tiere und Biotope für seltene Pflanzen.

The eastern Alps have been farmed for nearly 4,000 years. Today too, alpine pastures perform an invaluable function in the preservation of the ecological balance. Grazing prevents open areas from becoming overgrown, holds erosion at bay and reduces the danger of avalanches. Ecologically still intact, our alpine pastures provide precious recreational space, safe harbour for animals and biotopes for rare plant species.

Kranichberger Schwaig auf dem Wechsel | *Kranichberger Schwaig on Wechsel*

Hochgefühl

High Feelings

„Ein schmaler Pfad zwischen lockerem Kalkgeröll hängt über einen Abgrund von achthundert Klaftern hin … das Rollen des Kalkgruses unter den Füßen am unsicheren Rande des Abgrundes, alles erhöht hier die bangen Gefühle des Schwindels. Mit Entsetzen kehrt man das Auge hinweg von den grausenvollen Bildern …" (J. A. Schultes 1802, S. 138)
Da waren es ungefähr 20 Bergsteiger pro Jahr, die es wagten, den Schneeberg zu besteigen. Erst gegen Ende des 19. Jahrhunderts erschloss man alpintouristisch Wege, die nun mit sportlicher Begeisterung begangen werden. Schwierige Kletterrouten folgen zum Teil uralten Steigen von Jägern und Holzknechten und führen in hochalpine Bereiche, die Anfang des 19. Jahrhunderts „mit ihren schaudervollen Felsklippen" noch angstvoll gemieden worden waren.

"A narrow trail dangerously perched high above a sheer 800 m abyss winding through loose limestone gravel … the loose gravel underfoot so close to the unstable rim of the canyon, everything contributes to an uneasy feeling of vertigo. Terrified, you turn your eyes away from those images of danger …" (J. A. Schultes 1802, p.138).
Each year approximately 20 mountaineers dared to climb Schneeberg. It was only towards the end of the 19th century that the decision was made to construct alpine trails and climbing routes, which could henceforth be successfully hiked and climbed. Parts of the most challenging climbing trails followed the ancient trails of hunters and lumberjacks and led into high alpine territory, which people used to steer clear of due to its threatening cliffs.

Kletterer auf dem Geierstein oberhalb von Payerbach | *Rock climbers at the summit of Geierstein above Payerbach*

Blick auf Schottwien und Schneeberg | *View of Schottwien and Schneeberg*

Bergtouren um die Jahrhundertwende glichen Expeditionen: Mit Kindern, Dienstboten und Bergführern stieg man auf, Träger und Maultiere beförderten Körbe mit Wäsche, Proviant und Leckereien. Auf Alm- und Schutzhütten wurde übernachtet, um den Sonnenaufgang auf dem Gipfel zu erleben.
Schneeberg und Rax mit ihren Felswänden waren die Lieblingsberge der Wiener Bergsteiger, die an Samstagen auf dem Wiener Südbahnhof als „Haufen erbittert raxender Touristen in grimmig grandiosen Verkleidungen" (Hermann Bahr, Tagebuch, Berlin 1909) zu sehen waren. Bequeme Gäste ließen sich im „fauteuil-Alpenwagen", von Pferden gezogen, auf das Raxplateau kutschieren oder eroberten alpine Höhen mit der Schneeberg-Zahnradbahn und der Raxseilbahn. Man genoss den Bergsommer mit Spaziergängen und Jausen auf den Almen, mit Tennisspielen, Reiten und Radfahren (im Reichenauer Tal gab es eine eigene Fahrradordnung), Scheibenschießen und Schwimmen in Freibädern.
Heute ist manches anders – bestens ausgebaute Wanderwege und gesicherte Klettersteige, komfortable Hütten, Bergbahnen, Lifte und Straßen erschließen die Höhenregionen, modernste Sport- und Freizeitanlagen bieten alles, was das Herz begehrt. Spannende Erlebnisse warten, wenn man bereit ist, auf Entdeckungsreise zu gehen, Wiesen und Wälder zu durchstreifen, Spuren zu folgen und die Gegend mit all ihren Schönheiten zu erfahren, erradeln und ergehen. Ob man sich nach Ruhe und Abgeschiedenheit sehnt oder Abwechslung, Sport und Spaß sucht – die Möglichkeiten, hier in Bewegung zu kommen, sind so vielfältig wie die Landschaft selbst.

Around the turn of the century, hiking trips in the Alps resembled expeditions: together with a convoy of children, servants and guides one ascended, sherpas and mules carried baskets containing clothes, food and sweets for the children. One stayed overnight in an alpine cabin to observe the sunrise from the summit.
Schneeberg and Rax with their steep cliff faces used to be the favourites of Viennese mountaineers, who would appear on Saturdays at Vienna's southern railway station "like a heap of determined Rax tourists, all clad in strangely curious gear" to the eye of the beholder (Hermann Bahr, diary, Berlin 1909). The less active and hardy guests were transported up the mountain to the plateau in a horse drawn "fauteuil-Alpine" carriage, or they conquered the Alpine heights in the Schneeberg funicular and the Rax cableway. The mountain summer was whiled away in countless walking trips and snacking in the cabins, playing tennis, horseback riding and cycling (the Reichenau valley had its own bike rules), shooting, and swimming in open air pools. Today, quite a bit has changed – well maintained hiking trails and climbing routes, well equipped cabins, cableways, lifts and roads have all helped bring civilization to the higher regions, the latest state-of-the art sports and leisure parks offer anything you could ask for.
You are in for exciting experiences if you are ready to go on a discovery tour, saunter through meadows and woods, follow tracks and fully comprehend the area in all its stunning beauty, cycling or walking through it. Whether it is peace and quiet or sports, fun and a change every once in a while – the opportunities to get moving around here are as diverse as the surrounding landscape itself.

Blick vom Hochschneeberg ins Puchberger Tal und Gämse | *View of Hochschneeberg into Puchberg valley and Alpine goats*

König Schneeberg
King Schneeberg

Meine Eltern waren keine Bergfanatiker: Unsere durchschnittliche Familien-Wanderung dauerte fünf Minuten und führte vom Parkplatz beim Losenheimer Wasserfallwirt zum Wasserfall. Das nannten wir „Schneeberg-Wanderung". Dort angelangt, ließen wir Limo-Dosen um die Wette fahren – in den kleinen Seitenarmen des Wasserfall-Baches. So lernte ich von klein auf: „Der Schneeberg muss unendlich hoch sein, da kommt man nie im Leben rauf und am schönsten sind die Berge von unten."
Vielen ist ja das Wandern in der Kindheit vermiest worden: Durch Wander-Urlaube mit den Eltern oder durch Gewaltmärsche auf Schulwandertagen. Zwischen elf und zweiundzwanzig Jahren sind die meisten jungen Leute absolut resistent gegen Berge.
Aber mit dreiundzwanzig kommt plötzlich einer auf die Idee, man könnte das fünfjährige Maturajubiläum auf der Kienthalerhütte abhalten. Und so schleppt an einem Samstag Nachmittag eine verwegene Schar mit kaputten Turnschuhen zwei Fünf-Liter-Fässer Bier durch die Weichtalklamm.
Das ist nicht gerade der gemütlichste Anstieg auf den Schneeberg. Er besteht aus einem Mittelding zwischen Bach und Weg. Nass wird man sicher und es gibt Passagen, da waren wir froh, dass wir die ganz Dicken zu Hause gelassen haben. Nach der Übernachtung schafften wir den Gipfel schon rein konditionell nicht mehr und außerdem: So ein vorlautes Pack, wie wir damals waren, hätte der Schneeberg gar nicht raufgelassen.
Glauben Sie, der lässt jeden hinauf? Sicher nicht. Der Schneeberg ist ein König und keinesfalls demokratisch gesinnt. Stolz blickt er auf die normal Sterblichen herab. Wer ihm Respekt entgegenbringt, der darf sich ihm nähern. Wehe dem, der seinen Zorn weckt.
„Üben Sie einmal mit der Mamauwiese, bevor Sie den Gipfel stürmen wollen!", empfiehlt er etwas forsch. Das ist eine Tour – gut geeignet für die demokratische Familie. Einige fahren mit dem Lift, die Jungen rennen zu Fuß. Dann geht es rechterhand bergab und wenn man unten links abbiegt, kommt man zur Mamauwiese. Dort liegen echte Kühe in der Sonne und bei der Hütte bekommt man ein Glas kuhwarme Milch. Fragen Sie aber nicht, ob man hier mit Kreditkarte bezahlen kann! Kühe, die bequem in der Sonne liegen, sind übrigens ein hervorragender Anlass, um über Demokratie, soziale Gerechtigkeit und den Sinn des Lebens zu diskutieren. Als leichtere Kost empfiehlt sich dann zum Abschied der Tour eine Forelle beim Wasserfallwirt.
Aber beim Wasserfallwirt waren wir ja schon in der Kindheit! Und jetzt sind wir immer noch nicht am Gipfel gewesen? Also dann – Bergausrüstung anlegen, Handschuhe, Taschenlampe und Mütze einpacken! Regenschutz sowieso! Fadensteig, wir kommen!
Verständigen Sie Wind und Nebel, die stellen sich bestimmt pünktlich ein und Sie können dann mit Bergkompetenz protzen: „Was würden wir jetzt ohne Taschenlampe machen?"
Der Fadensteig ist ein flotter Anstieg und verdirbt einem die Lust aufs Diskutieren: Demokratie hin oder her, die Hoheit bittet zum Empfang, wir lassen uns nicht lumpen. Wir möchten wissen, wie die Welt von oben aussieht. Und bevor wir den Endspurt wagen, stärken wir uns auf der Fischerhütte mit geselchten Würsten und Radler. Dann wird noch kontrolliert: Haben wir alles dabei, um seiner Durchlaucht ehrfürchtig zu begegnen?
Der Anstieg zum Gipfelkreuz ist kurz, kann aber unangenehm werden: „Verzeihung, Euer Durchlaucht, heute bin ich durch und durch feucht." Auch das Licht zur Audienz müssen Sie sich wahrscheinlich selbst aufdrehen. Und nehmen Sie beim Gipfelgruß den Hut nicht ab, setzen Sie sich eine Mütze auf! Wenn Sie zur Begrüßung unbedingt ein „Shakehands" haben wollen, bitte, dann ziehen sie die Fäustlinge über. Fluchen Sie aber nicht. Andere wollten schummeln und sind mit der Zahnradbahn gefahren. Die haben es aber eben nur bis zur Kaiserin geschafft – zum Elisabethkirchlein.
Seien Sie also froh, dass Sie hier sind. Vor allem, wenn die Sonne scheint. Genießen Sie den Ausblick und sagen Sie nicht: „War eh halb so schlimm!" Solche Typen kann der König nicht leiden. Sagen Sie „Danke lieber König!", und verbeugen Sie sich still. Und wenn Sie unten sind, dann schauen Sie immer wieder respektvoll nach oben. Dann freut sich der Schneeberg und ist gut zu Ihnen. Fragen Sie meine Eltern, die machen das schon lange so.

Georg Bauernfeind

My parents never used to be mountain fanatics: our typical family outing lasted five minutes and led from the car park near the Waterfall Inn to the waterfall itself. This was known to us as the Schneeberg hike. Once we had reached our destination, we would drop fizzy drink cans into the side channels of the creek and race them in a fizzy drink can race. That is how I learnt about Schneeberg's immense height, and that there is no way of getting up there, and that the beauty of the mountains only reveals itself to the beholder at the bottom.
Hiking used to prove a nightmare in a lot of childhood memories: a family hiking holiday or forced power hikes at school. The age group of twelve to 22-year-olds is absolutely resistant to the lure of the mountains.
Once 23 though, the idea of celebrating a fifth graduation anniversary at the Kienthaler Cabin suddenly emerges. And so a hardy band of youngsters in threadbare sneakers lugs two five-litre beer barrels through Weichtalklamm.
This is not necessarily the most comfortable way up Schneeberg. The track is a blend of creek and trail. You are guaranteed to get wet and there are certain sections which are not for the faint-hearted, and we were happy to have left our pudgier friends at home. After a heavy night, our physical condition did not allow us to reach the summit and what's more: King Schneeberg would not have let such a pack of loudmouths go up it anyway.
Do you seriously believe Schneeberg allows everybody up? Definitely not. Schneeberg is a king and therefore certainly not democratically-minded. Proudly he looks down on ordinary forms of human life. Whoever approaches with great respect may proceed. But if you rouse the king's wrath, beware of his rage.
"Before you rush up the summit, you'd better practise your hiking skills up Mamauwiese first", he recommends somewhat sternly. This is a trip – extremely well suited to the democratic family. Some sit comfortably in a chairlift, the young ones race up. You turn right down the hill, hang a left at the bottom, and Mamauwiese spreads before you. Real cows lie there in the sun; a glass of fresh lukewarm cow milk awaits the hiker at the cabin. Don't even ask if you could pay using your plastic money! By the way, cows basking in the sun are the perfect reason for discussing democracy, social justice and the meaning of life. At the end of the tour, you are recommended to opt for something a little lighter – a delicious trout at the Waterfall Inn.
But we stayed at the Waterfall Inn when we were children! And we still haven't been all the way up Schneeberg? Well then – strap on the gear, gloves, flashlight and cap go into the backpack as well! Definitely include bad weather gear! Fadensteig, here we come! Get in touch with the wind and the mist, they're sure to be there on time, and then you can show your mountaineering skills: "Where would we be now without a flashlight?"
Fadensteig proves to be steep and spoils any wish for discussion: democracy or not, His Highness has called for an audience, and we have accepted his invitation. We want to know what the world looks like from up there. Before we set off on the final spurt up the summit, we feast on sausages and shandy at the Fischer hut. Quick check: do we have everything we need for a proper audience at the king's summit?
The final climb to the peak, marked by a cross, is short, yet it could turn nasty: "My apologies, Sire, today I am soaked through and through." You will probably even need to turn on the light for the audience yourself. And don't take off your hat when saluting at the top, put on a cap! If you absolutely insist on shaking hands, please put your gloves on. Whatever you do, don't curse. Others tried to cheat and cam up with the funicular. However, they have only reached the empress – the Elisabeth Chapel.
So, rejoice, and be happy that you have made it. Particularly when the sun is out. Treasure the moment, and don't say, "Well, it wasn't that bad after all!" It is people who say that kind of thing that the king cannot stand. Simply say, "Thank you so much, dear King!" and bow quietly. Once you have reached the bottom again, turn around and cast your eyes back up in respect. Then Schneeberg will be pleased with you and will be good to you in future. Just ask my parents, they've been doing this for a long time.

Georg Bauernfeind

S. 126/127: Marienkäfer auf Edelweiß | *P. 126/127: ladybird on edelweiss*

Am Weg auf die Rax | *En route up the Rax*

„Jedenfalls gehe ich in die Berge (wie andere in die Wüste), um mich zu sammeln auf einsamen Wanderungen, sagen wir über das Plateau der Rax.“ (Viktor E. Frankl, 1995, S. 28)

Es gab viele Gründe, die berühmte Forscher und Wissenschaftler in vergangener Zeit dazu brachten, in die Abgeschiedenheit der Berge zu gehen.
Viktor E. Frankl, weltberühmter Psychologe und Begründer der Logotherapie, verbrachte als begeisterter Bergsteiger viel Zeit in den Bergen nahe Wiens. Der Klettersport war seine Leidenschaft bis ins 80. Lebensjahr.

Die Touren in den Bergen waren für Frankl die einzige Zeit, in der er sich nicht mit seinen Büchern und Vorträgen beschäftigte. Dabei hat er alle seine wichtigen Entscheidungen getroffen. Es hieß sogar, dass ihm seine 27 Ehrendoktorate nicht so viel bedeuteten wie die drei schwierigen Klettersteige auf der Rax und dem Peilstein, die ihm zu Ehren von den Erstbegehern „Frankl-Steige“ getauft worden sind.

Raxplateau; Seite 132/133: Eingang zur Eng in Reichenau | *Rax plateau; p. 132/133: entrance to the Eng in Reichenau*

"In any case, I hike in the mountains (just as others hike around deserts) to find myself again on lonesome walks across the plateau of the Rax." (Viktor E. Frankl, 1995, p. 28)

There were many reasons why famous scientists and researchers used to seek the tranquillity and loneliness of the mountains. Viktor E. Frankl, a world-famous psychologist and founding father of logo therapy, spent a lot of time in the mountains near Vienna. Climbing was his passion well into his 80th year.

His trips to the mountains were the only time Frankl could work on his books and prepare talks. He would make all his crucial decisions on his walking trips. It is said that all his 27 honorary doctorates didn't mean as much to him as the three most challenging climbing routes on Rax and Peilstein, which have been named "Frankl Steige" in his honour by their discoverers.

„Hier gut angekommen"

Kaiserin Maria Theresia hatte 1752 in Österreich eine Militärakademie gegründet. Zum Zahlmeister dieser neuen Ausbildungsstätte für Offiziere wurde Jacob Anton Perthold bestellt, der in der Folge mit seiner Familie an den neuen Dienstort nach Wiener Neustadt übersiedeln musste. Nun war zur damaligen Zeit in der inmitten einer Sumpflandschaft gelegenen Stadt das Klima wenig erfreulich. Perthold suchte daher einen Erholungsort und fand ihn am Mühlhof bei Payerbach, welches damals zur Herrschaft Reichenau des Stiftes Neuberg gehörte. Es ist heute nicht mehr nachvollziehbar, was damals den Abt des Stiftes Neuberg dazu bewog, entgegen der gültigen Grundverkehrsregelungen einem Bürger der Stadt Wiener Neustadt Haus- und Grundbesitz zu verkaufen. Jedenfalls wurde am 30. November 1758 zwischen der Herrschaft Reichenau und dem Zahlmeister Perthold ein Kaufvertrag abgeschlossen, der ihm das fast öde Haus am Schwarzafluss überließ. Es wurde in dem Kaufvertrag ausdrücklich betont, dass er dieses Haus „vor sich und die Seinigen zur dann und wannigen Luftveränderung" herrichten wolle.

Damit dürfte wohl der Nachweis erbracht sein, dass sich die erste ländliche Sommerfrische des Ostalpenraumes im Reichenauer Tal befand und Payerbach-Reichenau als Wiege der Sommerfrische anzusehen ist.

Seit damals hat die Gegend um Reichenau ihre Anziehungskraft nicht verloren. Mitglieder des Kaiserhauses, das Großbürgertum, Künstler und Wissenschafter, aber auch „Kleine Leute" kamen zur Erholung hierher und bildeten eine bunte Sommergesellschaft. Viele davon hinterließen Spuren ihrer Anwesenheit, denen es wert ist nachzugehen.

Erzherzog Karl Ludwig (1833 bis 1896), der Bruder Kaiser Franz Josefs I., hatte mit der Villa Wartholz ein sommerliches Refugium geschaffen, welches er mit seiner Familie ab 1874 alljährlich mehrere Monate bewohnte. Tagebuchaufzeichnungen des Erzherzogs geben Einblick in das sommerliche Leben von Mitgliedern des Kaiserhauses:

4. Juni 1874: Fahrt nach Wartholz – allgemeine Freude in die wohltätige Luft zu kommen. Speisen im Thalhof; abends Gewitter.

7. Juni: Mit den älteren zwei Kindern (Erzherzog Franz Ferdinand und Erzherzog Otto) zu Fuß in die Kirche nach Reichenau. Abends Fahrt mit Maria Theresia (Gemahlin des Erzherzogs Karl Ludwig) nach Mühlhof bei Payerbach, wo der schöne Garten der Fürstin Arenberg ist. Da arbeiteten Maria Theresia und ich im Garten. Wir setzten uns – ein herrlicher Abend – köstliche Luft. Die beiden älteren Kinder ritten auf Mauleseln aus, Graf Coreth begleitete sie auf einem Esel.

11. Juni: In der Früh Gräfin Göß vom Payerbacher Bahnhof abgeholt. Maria Theresia und ich ritten, sie fuhr mit dem Wagen in die Villa. Um drei Uhr Essen. Dann mit der Gräfin in das Höllenthal – Maria Theresia kutschierte. Die älteren Kinder ritten uns mit ihren Herren nach. Schöner Abend beim Kaiserbrunnen.

28. Juli: Mit Franzi und Otto im Bad des Schönerer (Erbauer der Wien-Gloggnitzer-Eisenbahn). Zu Tisch hatten wir den Maler Angely, der bei seinem Schwiegervater Schönerer wohnt. Angely erzählte sehr interessant. Er war vor kurzem in Berlin, um den Kaiser von Deutschland und die Prinzessin Friedrich Karl von Preussen zu malen. Auch Professor Körner aus Graz war bei Tisch.

27. September: Rückkehr von den Manövern. Maria Theresia holte mich vom Bahnhof ab und kutschierte mich nach Hause. Gegen halb zwölf fuhren wir in größerer Gesellschaft zur Singerin. Dort speisten wir, es ging sehr lustig zu; man bewarf sich gegenseitig mit Mehl. Dann Fahrt zum Reißthal. Mit Maria Theresia blieb ich bei einem Bauernhaus sitzen; die anderen gingen zu Fuß weiter. Wieder zur Singerin – dort Kaffee und nach Hause.
28. September: Nach 12 Uhr nach Payerbach. Von dort mit dem Zug auf den Semmering. Von der Station ein Stück zu Fuß, dann mit den dort wartenden Wägen auf die Passhöhe über die alte Straße zum „Erzherzog Johann" an der steirischen Grenze. Dort Fleisch und Obst; Maria Theresia und die Kinder schaukelten. Mit den Wägen nach Maria Schutz. Wir gingen in die Kirche und fuhren dann nach Schottwien. Maria Theresia und Baronin Walterskirchen gingen zu Fuß. Wir warteten auf sie. Sie brachte einen großen Hund mit, den ihr die Witwe des Taschenspielers Döbler, die bei Maria Schutz ein Haus hat, schenkte. Zu Hause am Abend zur Freude der Kinder „Schwarzer Peter" gespielt.
29. September: Auf der großen Wiese vor der Villa stand ein Heuwagen auf den wir (Maria Theresia und die anderen) mit einer Leiter stiegen und öfters herunter rutschten. Zu Fuß mit Maria Theresia nach Reichenau an der Villa Szechenyi vorbei wieder nach Hause. Abends spielte Kapellmeister Eder Klavier und Harmonium. Maria Theresia und auch andere spielten Klavier. Ich tanzte ein paar Touren mit Maria Theresia.
30. September: Mit Wägen in die Adlitzgräben. Am Ende zu Fuß weiter – Wägen fuhren zurück. Bei einem Bauern in der Nähe des Ortbauern Milch, Butter, Honig und Brot gegessen. Weiter nach Prein – von dort mit Wagen nach Hause. Abends getanzt.
3. Oktober: Abreise nach Ischl.
Als typischer Vertreter des Großbürgertums war durch mehr als 50 Jahre der Richter des Oberlandesgerichtes Alfred Pick in der Reichenauer Sommergesellschaft anzutreffen. Er war der Sohn des Juristen Gustav Pick, der als Dichter und Komponist des Fiakerliedes bekannt war. In dem schmalen autobiographischen Bändchen „Ich über mich", welches 1915 erschien, beschrieb er auch die alljährlichen Sommeraufenthalte in Reichenau:
„Als ganz kleines Kind war ich zum ersten mal (1871) hier und seither bin ich 44 Jahre lang wiedergekommen, in jeden Jahr manchmal auf kürzere, manchmal auf längere Zeit; nie war ich untreu! Wir waren damals viele Familienmitglieder und einmal bewohnten wir im Thalhof 13 Zimmer. Auch viele Freunde besuchten uns hier, es herrschte ein ewiges Kommen und Gehen. Mein Vater nahm immer sein Klavier und sein Harmonium mit heraus und jeden Sonntag wurde musiziert. Die Holzknechte sangen bei meinem Vater, er spielte dazu Klavier und meine Tante Dora Zither.
Von den Gästen des Thalhofes aus jener Zeit ist mir besonders Baron Haertl, der so hübsche Gedichte machte, in Erinnerung geblieben. Zu den Gästen gehörte auch der prächtige Lavossy, der eigentlich Polifka hieß, früher in Reichenau Gendarm war, dann die reiche Hofschneiderin Breier heiratete und ein reizendes Holzhaus aus Schweden kommen ließ, das heute noch hoch über der Straße zum Thalhof steht.
Auch meine bescheidenen Jagderlebnisse standen mit dem Reichenauer Thalhof in Verbindung: Als ich einmal mit einem erlegten Hasen beladen, stolz in den Thalhof einmarschierte, erblickte mich Erzherzog Franz Ferdinand und fragte den Zahlkellner, wer ich denn sei. Dieser antwortete: ‚Der junge Pick' und fügte erklärend hinzu: ‚Na der Sohn vom Komponisten Gustav Pick'. Das war meine Bekanntschaft mit einer kaiserlichen Hoheit."
Von vielen Menschen aus einfachen Verhältnissen, die auch im Raxgebiet Erholung suchten, haben sich in der Regel nur Ansichtskarten im Stil von „Hier gut angekommen, das Wetter ist schön", oder mit einem ähnlichen Text erhalten. Bisher konnte nur eine einzige Ansichtskarte gefunden werden, die darüber hinaus über die Bedürfnisse einer Urlauberin, die wahrscheinlich aus dem Arbeiterstand kam und sich in die Sommergesellschaft einfügen wollte, Aufschluss gibt. Die Karte wurde von einer jungen Mutter geschrieben, die 1910 mit ihrer Tochter in Edlach zur Erholung war: „Liebste Mutter! Sei so gut und schicke mir per Post nachstehende Sachen; und zwar, den gestreiften Barchentunterrock, eine Barchenthose, die schwarze Reformhose, die weiße Panamablouse, ein Nachtkorsett, ein Miederleibl, zwei Paar Strümpfe, einen Hutnadelschützer. Und für die Kleine kaufe ein kleines Deckerl zum Ausnähen – Kreuzelstich, und Wolle dazu, aber nur was sehr billiges. Also bitte liebe Mutter sei lieb und schicke mir die Sachen recht bald. Gruß Josefine."

Robert Pap

"Arrived safely"

Empress Maria Theresa of Austria founded a military academy in 1752. The position of purser at this brand new training site for officers was given to Jacob Anton Perthold, who as a consequence had to move his family to Wiener Neustadt, his new posting. The climate in Wiener Neustadt used to be extremely unpleasant, for the town was surrounded by a swampy landscape. Perthold therefore looked for a place for recreation and found the Mühlhof in Payerbach, which back then was part of Reichenau, owned by Neuberg monastery. It is hard to reconstruct the reasons why the abbot decided to sell the house and plot of land to a citizen of Wiener Neustadt, which was against all the existing ownership rules. In any case, a contract between the monastery and purser Perthold for the rather run-down house by the Schwarza River was signed on November 30, 1758. The contract clearly stated that the property would be refurbished and renovated for the sole purpose of allowing him and his family to enjoy an occasional change of scenery.

This contract is proof that summer tourism in the eastern Alps was in fact born in the Reichenau valley and Payerbach-Reichenau.

Ever since then, the region surrounding Reichenau has kept its appeal for visitors. Members of the royal court, middle class commoners, artists and scientists, but also "ordinary people" visited this region for recreational purposes and thus formed a very mixed summertime party. Many of them left evidence of their presence that are worthwhile following up on.

Archduke Karl Ludwig (1833–1896), the brother of Emperor Franz Josef I, created a summer retreat at Villa Wartholz, where he and his family lived for a few months each year as of 1874. The archduke's entries in his diary reveal the happy summers members of the court spent here:

June 4th, 1874: drive out to Wartholz – everyone was delighted finally to get out into the clean air. Dinner at Thalhof; evening thunderstorm.

June 7th: walked to church in Reichenau with the older children (Archduke Franz Ferdinand and Archduke Otto). Evening trip with Maria Theresa (wife of Archduke Karl Ludwig) to Mühlhof near Payerbach, visited the stunning garden of Princess Arenberg. There, Maria Theresa and I did some gardening. We sat down – a glorious evening – delicious air. The two older children went for a ride on mules, Count Coreth accompanied them on a donkey.

June 11th: picked up Countess Göss at the train station in Payerbach. Maria Theresa and I rode back, the Countess got a lift back to the villa in the carriage. Afterwards Maria Theresa drove the horse drawn carriage into the Höllental, with Countess Göss and me. The older children followed us, accompanied by their lords. Nice evening near Kaiserbrunn.

July 28th: relaxed with Franzi and Otto at Schönerer's pool (construction engineer of the Vienna-Gloggnitz railway). We had the painter Angely over for lunch, who is staying with Schönerer, his father-in-law. Angely told some interesting stories. A short while ago he was in Berlin to paint the emperor of Germany and Prince Friedrich Karl of Prussia. Professor Körner from Graz lunched with us as well.

September 27th: return from manoeuvres. Maria Theresa picked me up at the station and drove me home. Around half past

eleven we went out to the Singerin with a big crowd. There we lunched, it was a lot of fun, with a flour fight. Subsequently drove to the Reissthal. Maria Theresa and I stayed at a farmhouse; the others walked on. Back to the Singerin – we had coffee there and returned later.
September 28th: after noon, went to Payerbach. Caught the train to Semmering. Had to walk a little to reach the carriages, which then carried us up along the old road to the Semmering Pass, where had something to eat at the "Erzherzog Johann" at the Styrian border. We had meat and fruit; Maria Theresa and the children played on a seesaw. Went by carriage down to Maria Schutz. Looked inside the church and then drove on to Schottwien. Maria Theresa and Baroness Walterskirchen walked to Schottwien. We waited for them. They had a large dog in tow, which was given to M.T. by the puppeteer Döbler's widow, who owns a house near Maria Schutz. Played "Black Peter" at home that night, much to our children's enjoyment.
September 29th: there was a hay wagon in the large meadow by the villa, which we climbed up and slid down a few times (Maria Theresa and the others). Walked to Reichenau with Maria Theresa, passed Villa Szechenyi and back again. Evening piano and harmonica concert by bandleader Eder. Maria Theresa and others played piano too. Danced a few times with Maria Theresa.
September 30th: went to the Adlitzgräben by carriage. Carried on walking for the last part. Carriages returned home. Ate milk, butter, honey and bread at a farmer's near Ortbauern. On to Prein – there we climbed into the carriages again and were driven home. Evening dancing.
October 3rd: left for Bad Ischl.
A typical representative of the middle class, judge Alfred Pick belonged to the Reichenau summer party for over 50 years. He was the son of the lawyer Gustav Pick, who was a famous writer and composer of the cabby song. In his autobiographic booklet "I on myself" (appeared in 1915) he describes the annual summer sojourns in Reichenau:
"I came here for the first time as a small child (1871), and I have been back for the past 44 years; sometimes for longer, other times shorter stays. Not a single year did I miss. Back then we used to be a large family, and one time we occupied 13 rooms at Thalhof. Many friends of the family visited us during our stays here, a permanent flux of people coming and going. My father brought his piano and accordion along, and each Sunday we would play music. The lumberjacks would sing songs, accompanied by my father's piano and my aunt's zither.
Of all the guests at Thalhof back then, I remember Count Haertl, who was a very talented poet, particularly well. Another guest was the great Polifka alias Lavossy, who used to be a policeman in Reichenau and who later married the wealthy tailor at the royal court, Ms. Breier, and had a lovely wooden house transported from Sweden; it is still perched neatly, high above the road to Thalhof.
Even my humble experiences of hunting were connected with Thalhof. Once I was proudly marching in Thalhof, with a rabbit I had killed on my shoulder. Archduke Franz Ferdinand spotted me and asked the waiter who I was. He replied, 'the young Pick', adding by way of explanation, 'the composer Gustav Pick's son'. And that was my experience with a member of the royalty."
Many less wealthy people visiting the region for recreation are remembered only from picture postcards with words such as "arrived safely, weather is nice" or something along these lines. Only one postcard has been discovered that offers more insight into the needs of a female holidaymaker – most probably of the working class – trying to keep up with the summer party. The card was written by a young mother holidaying in Edlach in 1910: "Dearest Mother! Please, be so kind as to mail me the striped barchent underskirt, the barchent trousers. the black reform trousers, the white blouse, a nightgown, a bodice, two pairs of stockings and a hatpin protector. And buy a small blanket for the little one for me embroider – cross-stitch and wool, but something very cheap. Well, dear mother, please forward these things to me as soon as possible. Love, Josefine."

Robert Pap

„Wir steigen aus. Wir atmen rasiermesserscharfe Bergluft ein. Wir sind geborgen im Waldesfrieden. Hinter uns der Dunst des Getümmels, Getriebes." (Peter Altenberg, Semmering 1912)

Kletschkahöhe in Reichenau | *Kletschkahöhe in Reichenau*

"We get off. Instantly, we breathe in razor-sharp mountainous air. We're at ease in the tranquillity of the forest. Behind us lies the haze of the congested, the hurly burly." (Peter Altenberg, Semmering 1912)

Payerbach am Schwarzafluss bei Tag und Nacht | *Payerbach at the Schwarza River by day and by night*

Heilung und Regeneration mit den Kräften der Natur haben in der Region eine lange Tradition, die bis ins 19. Jahrhundert zurückreicht. Die Bergwelt von Schneeberg, Rax, Semmering und Wechsel, der „gesunde Lungenflügel Wiens", mit Licht, Sonne und guter Luft, war die Alternative zum Leben in der Großstadt, die immer lauter, schmutziger und schnelllebiger wurde. Die Stadt schlug sich nicht nur aufs Gemüt, sondern auch auf die Gesundheit. Jene, die es sich leisten konnten, suchten in den Bergen Erholung.
In Tourismusprospekten der Jahrhundertwende wurden die Milde und der Ozonreichtum der Höhenluft, die den Appetit förderte und die Nerven beruhigte, mit medizinischen Gutachten empfohlen. Hotels, Kuranstalten und Sanatorien boten schon damals Heilungs- und Erholungsaufenthalte auch in elegantem Rahmen.
Bergbahnen ermöglichten die Wirkung einer Klimaschaukel zwischen mildem Reizklima und hochalpinem Klima. Kaltwasserbehandlungen, Freiluftliegekuren, Sport-, Bewegungs- und Sonnenlichttherapien in Höhenlagen wurden Sommer und Winter über als Heil- und Verjüngungsmittel und als neuer Weg zu einer natürlichen und naturnahen Lebensweise angeboten.
Heilung und Regeneration mit den Kräften der Natur stehen auch heute bei den Kuren im Vordergrund. Es gibt viele Schätze, die die Natur hier jedem zur Verfügung stellt, der sie sucht: die Schönheit der Bergwelt, in der man zur Ruhe und in Bewegung kommt; Wasser, das in klaren Quellen zu Tage tritt, das erfrischend, heilend und belebend wirkt und hilft, wieder zum Ursprung zu gelangen; die Bergluft, in der man wieder durchatmen kann. Ausgedehnte Wälder und das Umweltbewusstsein der Menschen hier sorgen für eine hervorragende Luftqualität; die Pflanzen und Kräuter, aus denen man in Heubädern Kraft und Gesundheit tanken und den Körper entgiften und entschlacken kann; die Früchte und Produkte der Natur als Basis für eine gesunde Naturküche sowie spezielle Diäten und Kuren.

Schloss Gloggnitz bei Tag und Nacht | *Gloggnitz Castle by day and by night*

Healing and regeneration using the power of nature boast a long tradition in this region, dating back to the 19th century. The alpine world of Schneeberg, Rax, Semmering and Wechsel, "Vienna's intact lungs", offering light, sun and pristine air, has always offered an alternative to city life, which has been picking up pace, becoming noisier and dirtier. Not only did life in the city affect one's state of mind and mood, it also affected one's physical health. Those could afford it headed for the mountains to recharge their batteries.

Mild alpine air, rich in ozone, sparking one's appetite and calming one's nerves, was recommended by medical experts and advertised in tourist brochures around the turn of the century. Hotels, spas and sanatoria offered convalescence and recreational stays in a rather exquisite environment.

Lifts enabled one to enjoy the effects of the seesaw of a mild and high alpine climate. Cold water treatments, open air health cures, sports, activity and sunlight therapies in winter and summer in the higher regions were offered as a means of reaching a natural lifestyle close to nature. Today too, natural powers above all are applied in healing and regeneration cures. Nature offers an abundance of treasures to anyone who searches for and is willing to accept them:

the beauty of the alpine world, which allows one to calm down and get moving; untouched water springing to life offering unparalleled refreshment and healing and helps you to return to your roots; alpine air letting you breathe again. Extensive forests and the environmental awareness of the local inhabitants ensure excellent air quality; plants and herbs decontaminate your body and let your power cells and health recharge in hay baths; the fruits and produce of nature provide the basis for natural cuisine as well as special dietary requirements and weight loss regimens.

Die Straße nach dem Süden

The Road Leading South

Der Semmeringpass war zugleich Verbindung und Barriere auf dem wichtigen Handelsweg von Wien nach dem Süden. Es war daher stets ein besonderes Anliegen der Landesherren, die Straße über den Semmering in einem möglichst guten Zustand zu erhalten und einem gesteigerten Verkehr anzupassen. Meist entsprachen aber die vorhandenen Staatsmittel nicht diesem Bestreben, so dass Kaiser Karl VI. an den Landesgrenzen, aber auch an den Vorstadtlinien Wiens einen Kreuzer pro Zugtier für diesen Zweck einheben ließ. Nun war es möglich, die Straße über den Semmering neu zu trassieren. Sie wurde 1728 fertiggestellt, woran ein auf der Passhöhe errichtetes prunkvolles Denkmal erinnert. Der damals bestehenden Lehre der Straßenbaukunst entsprechend, war sie aber so steil angelegt, dass bei großen Frachtwagen drei bis vier Paar schwerer Pferde vorgespannt werden mussten, um sie auf die Höhe des Semmeringpasses zu schaffen. Vor diesem schwierigen Straßenstück wurde meist in Schottwien genächtigt. Dort waren dann die breitfelgigen Kaufmannswagen auf dem Ortsplatz abgestellt und von riesigen Hunden bewacht. Während die Kutscher und Fuhrknechte die zahlreichen Wirtshäuser bevölkerten, übernahmen die tagsüber lammfrommen Hunde die Wacht bei den Wagen. Wehe, wenn sich ein Fremder diesen näherte, die schwarzzotteligen Ungeheuer zwangen ihn zu sofortigem Rückzug. Auch wenn sich der Pfarrherr von Schottwien über die vielen Exzesse, Rohheiten und Unsittlichkeiten beklagte, damals regierte dank des Vorspanngeschäftes der Gulden in Schottwien.

Wurde auch die Straße über den Semmering als besondere technische Leistung von den Zeitgenossen gepriesen, so war sie doch mit vielen Unzulänglichkeiten behaftet und dem Verkehr des beginnenden 19. Jahrhunderts nicht mehr gewachsen. Damals versäumte es der Kreisingenieur Johann Michael Baumgartner durch 30 Jahre kein einziges Mal, den Kaiser bei jeder Reise über den Semmering zu begleiten und, mit den ausgearbeiteten Plänen in der Hand, auf den dringend notwendigen „kunstmäßigen" Ausbau der Bergstraße hinzuweisen. Erst 1839 war es dann so weit, dass dem Bauunternehmer Felix Tallachini aus Varese in der Provinz Como der Neubau der Semmeringstraße übertragen wurde. Über den Bau schreibt der Pfarrer der Wallfahrtskirche in Maria Schutz: „Dieser kolossale Bau hat gleich im ersten Jahr zwischen ein- bis zweitausend Arbeiter beiderlei Geschlechts und Alters und von verschiedenen Ländern, teilweise Italiener, größtenteils aber Böhmen herbeigezogen. Dass dadurch auch sehr viele Vagabunden und liederliches Gesindel herbeigelockt und die größten Unordnungen und Exzesse veranlasst wurden, versteht sich von selbst. Das gedrängte Zusammenwohnen ohne Unterschied des Geschlechts in Erdhöhlen und bretternen Baracken leisten der Unzucht vielen Vorschub und die heillosen Branntwein-Saufgelage und die infolge der Völlerei entstandenen Schlägereien und Raufhändel übersteigen alle Grenzen. Viele Arbeiter büßen ihr Leben bei diesem Bau ein, teils infolge der von schlechter Lebensart und Pflege entstandenen Krankheiten, teils durch Unglücksfälle bei den Erdarbeiten; teils haben sich mehrere im wahrsten Sinn des Wortes tot gesoffen."

Trotz dieser Schwierigkeiten konnte die neue Straße über den Semmering am 17. August 1841 von Kaiser Ferdinand I. mit einer Fahrt im sechsspännigen Reisewagen eröffnet werden. Sie war nach allen Regeln der „französischen Straßenbaukunst" angelegt und stieg in sechs weitgezogenen Serpentinen zur Passhöhe an, so dass man bergauf mit einem Pferdewagen im Trab fahren konnte und bergab weder Radschuh noch Sperrkette brauchte. Diese Straße war gerade rechtzeitig fertig geworden, um ab 1844 bis zur Fertigstellung der Semmeringbahn den sprunghaft angewachsenen Verkehr zwischen den Bahnhöfen Gloggnitz und Mürzzuschlag zu übernehmen. Musste damals doch jeder Reisende und jedes Frachtstück mit Pferdewagen zwischen diesen vorläufigen Endpunkten der südlichen Staatsbahn über den Semmering gebracht werden. Aber auch nach Eröffnung der Semmeringbahn behielt die Straße ihre Bedeutung, denn die Trassierung war so geglückt, dass sie später ohne Umbauten auch dem modernen Autoverkehr entsprach.

Semmering Pass served both as a link and a barrier along the major trading route leading south from Vienna. Constant maintenance and improvement of the road over Semmering used to be one of the monarchs' highest priorities. Unfortunately, financial resources did not always allow for proper upkeep, and Emperor Karl VI therefore introduced a toll of 1 kreutzer per draught animal, both at the provincial and the city boundary. It was this that made the road's new layout possible. The 1728 completion date is preserved in a grand monument at the Semmering Pass. Since the gradient of the road was so steep, three to four pairs of draught horses were required to tow heavy loads up the incline. Schottwien became a rest stop before travellers tackled the mountain pass. The village square served as a gigantic tradesmen's carriage park protected by large dogs. While the coachmen ate and drank at one of the many inns at night, the dogs – perfectly docile during the day – would keep a sharp eye on the heavy carriages. If anybody dared approach the carts, the dogs would instantly drive them back without much ado. Even though the minister of Schottwien would complain about the many excesses, rude and inappropriate behaviour, money had the bigger say in Schottwien than the minister's word.

Despite the generally good opinion of the road over Semmering – it was considered a technical masterpiece – it was nonetheless inadequate for the constantly increasing traffic at the beginning 19th century. In those days, in 30 years regional engineer Johann Michael Baumgartner never missed an opportunity to accompany the emperor each time he used the pass and point out that the mountain road was in urgent need of complete and thorough overhaul. 1839 saw the reconstruction of the road across the Semmering, carried out by entrepreneur Felix Tallachini from Varese in the Italian province of Como. The minister of Maria Schutz pilgrimage church wrote of the project: "This enormous construction project drew between one and two thousand workers, male and female, young and old, from many different nations, partly Italians, mostly Bohemians though, in the first year on site. It goes without saying that this grand project also drew many vagabonds and dubious types and triggered off a great deal of unruly and excessive behaviour. Living literally on top of each other in the most basic and humble forms of accommodation generated low morale and mindless drinking; as a result, brutal fighting and reckless violence spread amongst the working population. Many workers lost their lives on this site, due in part to the poor and primitive sanitation but also to excessive drinking and sheer violence, only some of which were accidents on the job; some literally drank themselves into their graves."

Despite all these difficulties, the new road across Semmering was opened on August 17, 1841 by Emperor Ferdinand I, travelling in a grand horse-drawn carriage. The road was laid according to the latest French road-building principles and wound its way up in six sweeping switchbacks, enabling horse drawn carriages to race up Semmering; coming down neither chain block nor wheel block were required. The road was completed just in time to handle the increased traffic between the train stations of Gloggnitz and Mürzzuschlag from 1844 until Semmering railway was completed. In those days, every traveller and piece of luggage had to be hauled over the mountain pass on horseback, between the temporary terminals of the Southern State Railway Line. Even after the Semmering railway was opened, the importance of the road never faded, as the road was built to last and handle modern traffic as well.

Robert Pap

Ruine Klamm, Semmeringbahn und Klosterwappen, rechts die Semmeringbahn am Eichberg vor dem Raxpanorama
The Ruins of Klamm Castle, Semmering railway and coat of arms, Semmering railway at Eichberg with panoramic views of the Rax in the background

Semmeringbahn & umgebende Landschaft

Semmering railway & surrounding landscape

Die Semmeringbahn – über 41 km lange Gebirgsbahn, von 1848 bis 1854 erbaut – ist eine der größten Ingenieursleistungen der Pionierzeit des Eisenbahnbaues. Der hohe Standard der Tunnels, Viadukte und der weiteren Bauten hat bis heute den Eisenbahnbetrieb ermöglicht. Die Trasse führt durch eine imposante Berglandschaft, in der Villen und Sommersitze entstanden, als der Tourismus durch die Erschließung der Landschaft in Folge der Bahneröffnung erblühte.

Semmering railway, built over 41 km of high mountains between 1848 and 1854, is one of the greatest feats of civil engineering from this pioneering period of railway building. The high standard of the tunnels, viaducts and other structures has ensured continuous use of the railway to this day. It runs through spectacular mountain landscape, and there are many fine buildings designed for leisure activities along the way, built when the area was opened up following the advent of the railway.

UNESCO Weltkulturerbe Semmeringbahn und umgebende Landschaft | *UNESCO World Heritage Semmering railway and surrounding landscape*

Semmeringbahn: Österreich, 41 km, von Gloggnitz nach Mürzzuschlag, Niederösterreich und Steiermark 15°40'8"E,47°36'7"N – 15°56'3"E,47°40'46"N

Semmering railway: Austria, 41 km, Gloggnitz to Mürzzuschlag, provinces of Lower Austria and Styria 15°40'8"E,47°36'7"N – 15°56'3"E,47°40'46"N

Blick über das Südbahnhotel auf dem Semmering und weitere österreichische Welterbestätten: Schloss Schönbrunn, Wachau, Salzburg Altstadt, Wien Innenstadt

View of Semmering with the Südbahn Hotel in the foreground and further Austrian sites on the World Heritage List: Schönbrunn Palace, Wachau, Salzburg Old City, Inner City of Vienna

Welterbestätten

World heritage sites

„Werke von Menschenhand oder gemeinsame Werke der Natur und des Menschen sowie Gebiete, einschließlich archäologischer Stätten, die in historischer, ästhetischer, ethnologischer oder anthropologischer Hinsicht von außergewöhnlichem universellem Wert sind."

In Österreich sind Schloss und Park Schönbrunn sowie die Altstadt von Salzburg seit 1997, die Kulturlandschaft Hallstatt-Dachstein/Salzkammergut seit 1998, die Semmeringbahn und umgebende Landschaft seit 1999 und die Altstadt von Graz seit dem Jahr 2000 in die Welterbeliste eingetragen, ebenso die Wachau und der Neusiedlersee. Weitere Einreichungen sind vorgesehen.

"Works of man or the combined works of nature and man, and areas including archaeological sites which are of outstanding universal value from the historical, aesthetic, ethnological or anthropological point of view."

Schönbrunn Palace and its gardens and the old city of Salzburg have been listed as world cultural heritage sites since 1997, the cultural landscape of Hallstatt-Dachstein / Salzkammergut since 1998, the Semmering railway and the surrounding countryside since 1999, and the old city of Graz along with the Wachau region and Lake Neusiedl since the year 2000. Further Austrian sites will be submitted in the future.

Über die Grenzen hinaus
Beyond Borders

Was verbindet die Ghega-Semmeringbahn mit Stonehenge, den Pyramiden Ägyptens oder dem Kolosseum Roms? – Sie stehen auf der von der UNESCO geführten Liste des Welterbes und sind Kulturzeugnisse und einzigartige Naturlandschaften, deren Untergang ein unersetzlicher Verlust für die gesamte Menschheit wäre. Sie zu schützen liegt also nicht allein in der Verantwortung des Einzelnen, sondern ist Aufgabe der Völkergemeinschaft.

What do the Ghega Semmering railway, Stonehenge, the Egyptian pyramids and the Coliseum in Rome have in common? They are all on the World Heritage List maintained by UNESCO and are the products of culture or unique natural landscapes the loss of which would represent an irreplaceable loss for all mankind. Their protection is therefore not the duty of the individual but of all nations.

Welterbefeier beim Viadukt Kalte Rinne (Semmeringbahn) und Stonehenge (Südengland)
World Heritage festivities at the Kalte Rinne viaduct (Semmering railway) and Stonehenge (southern England)

Galerie der Semmeringbahn in der Weinzettlwand und Kreuzgang des Klosters Quyn Abbey in Irland
Semmering Railway: Weinzettlwand Gallery and cloisters of Quyn Abbey in Ireland

Schon im Mittelalter eröffnete dieses Kloster in Irland den Mönchen durch neue Erfahrungen in Wissenschaft und Glauben einen Horizont über die Grenzen der Insel hinaus.
Die Semmeringbahn, seit 1854 erste Gebirgsbahn der Welt von Wien auf den Semmering, gab denen, die sich auf die Reise machten, nicht nur neue Ausblicke in die wilde Landschaft. Sie erschloss eine neue Welt über die bisherigen Grenzen hinaus.

Even back in medieval times, this monastery in Ireland expanded the horizons of its residents far beyond the borders of the island with new insights gained in science and belief.
Semmering Railway, since 1854 the world's foremost mountain railway connecting Vienna and the Semmering, not only offered the traveller stunning vistas of untouched landscapes but also opened up new worlds reaching beyond known boundaries.

Der Schneeberg spiegelt sich im Schmelzwasser, der Ayers Rock im Wüstensee
Schneeberg reflected in a freshwater lake, Ayers Rock in a desert lake

Durchreist man das 1.000.000 m² große Wüstengebiet von Australien, das Neverneverland, taucht am Horizont der Ayers Rock, der größte Felsen der Welt, auf. Und es dauert noch Stunden, bis man ihn erreicht hat.

Von der weit mehr als 1.000.000 Einwohner großen Hauptstadt Österreichs sieht man an klaren Tagen den Schneeberg am Horizont. Hier beginnen auch die Alpen, Europas größte Gebirgskette. Von Wien in nur einer Stunde erreichbar.

Travellers crossing the 1,000,000 m² of desert in Australia's interior, the Never Never Land, will see the world's largest monolith, Ayers Rock, on the horizon. Yet it takes hours before they finally get there.

On clear, sunny days, the population of Austria's capital city Vienna, numbering more than 1,000,000, can catch a glimpse of Schneeberg on the horizon. This is the beginning of the Alps, Europe's most extensive mountain range, less than an hour's drive away.

Roggenfeld in der Buckligen Welt und Welle im pazifischen Ozean
Undulating field of barley in Bucklige Welt and wave in the Pacific Ocean

Die Sehnsucht nach Unendlichkeit lässt uns stundenlang am Meer sitzen und in der Sonne das Spiel der Wellen betrachten. Unsere Ozeane sind die Getreidefelder, die Wasser aufnehmen, in der Sonne leuchten und sich im Wind wiegen.
Und wer still ist, hört das Rauschen und mehr …

Our longing for eternity makes us sit for endless hours on the sea shore, watching the ceaseless play of the waves, rolling and crashing in the sun. Our oceans are cornfields, which take up water, glisten in the sun and ripple in the wind.
Those who make no noise will hear the rushing sound and more …

Literatur

B i b l i o g r a p h y

Peter Altenberg: Extrakte des Lebens – Gesammelte Skizzen 1898–1919. Hg. W. J. Schweiger. Wien, Frankfurt 1987.

Peter Altenberg: Vita ipsa. Berlin 1918.

Peter Baumgartner: Kleine Bucklige Welt. Wien 1984.

Robert Bouchal, Josef Wirth: Österreichs faszinierende Höhlenwelt. Wien 2000.

Georg Brandstätter: Naßwald und seine Pioniere. Ternitz – Pottschach 1998.

Georg Brandstätter: Die Rax. Ternitz – Pottschach 2001.

Heimito von Doderer: Die Strudlhofstiege oder Melzer und die Tiefe der Jahre. München 1985.

Franz Xaver Embel: Fußreise von Wien nach dem Schneeberge. Wien 1801.

Franz Xaver Embel: Schilderung der Gebirgs-Gegenden um den Schneeberg in Österreich. Wien 1803.

Viktor E. Frankl: Was nicht in meinen Büchern steht. Lebenserinnerungen. München 1995.

Johannes Gans: Wandererlebnis Bucklige Welt. St. Pölten – Wien 1995.

Wolfgang Haider-Berky: Sagen aus der Buckligen Welt. Neunkirchen o. J.

Wolfgang Haider-Berky: Sagen aus dem niederösterreichischen Wechselgebiet. Neunkirchen o. J.

Felix Halmer: Burgen und Schlösser Bucklige Welt, Semmering, Rax. Wien 1969.

Barbara Higgs, Wolfgang Straub (Hg.): Wegen der Gegend. Literarische Reisen durch Niederösterreich. Frankfurt 1997.

Thomas Hofmann: Sagenhaftes Niederösterreich. Eine Spurensuche zwischen Mythos und Wahrheit. Wien 2000.

Ottokar Janetschek: Der Raxkönig. Wien 1959, 1984.

Wolfgang Kos (Hg.): Die Eroberung der Landschaft. Semmering-Rax-Schneeberg. Katalog zur Niederösterreichischen Landesausstellung Schloss Gloggnitz 1992. Wien 1992.

Wolfgang Kos, Elke Krasny (Hg.): Schreibtisch mit Aussicht. Österreichische Schriftsteller auf Sommerfrische. Wien 1995.

Kunst- und Kulturkreis Stift Geras (Hg.): Geraser Hefte Nr. 19. 1988.

Willibald Leeb: Sagen Niederösterreichs. Wien 1892.

Karl Lukan: Herrgottsitz und Teufelsbett. Wien 1979.

Karl Lukan: Weißer Stein und Rotes Türl. Wien 1990.

Karl Lukan: Seltsame Kultstätten – Sonderbare Heilige. Kulturhistorische Wanderungen in Österreich. Wien 1995.

Karl Lukan: Schneeberg und Rax. Wien 1978.

Karl Lukan: Das Voralpenbuch. Wien, München 1986.

Marktgemeinde Hochneukirchen-Gschaidt (Hg.): Festschrit 700 Jahre Hochneukirchen. Hochneukirchen 1995.

Heinrich Mose: Aus der Waldmark. Neunkirchen 1904.

Heinrich Mose: Führer durch Gloggnitz und seine malerische Umgebung. Wr. Neustadt o. J.

Robert Pap: Wiedergefundenes Paradies. Sommerfrischen zwischen Reichenau und Semmering. Reichenau 1996.

Robert Pap: Reichenauer Spaziergänge. Ternitz – Pottschach 1998.

Adolf Schmidl: Der Schneeberg in Unterösterreich mit seinen Umgebungen von Wien bis Mariazell. Wien 1831.

Philipp Schoeller: Dörfles und Strelzhof. Chronik. Dörfles 1990.

Joseph August Schultes: Ausflüge nach dem Schneeberge in Unterösterreich. Wien 1802, Nachdruck Wien 1982.

Norbert Toplitsch: Sagen und Geschichten aus dem Semmering-Rax-Schneeberggebiet. Hg. Franz Prüger. Payerbach 1983.

Franz Carl Weidmann: Alpengegenden Niederösterreichs und Obersteyermarks im Bereiche der Eisenbahn von Wien bis Mürzzuschlag. Wien 1871 (5. Auflage).

Der einzige Skorpion in unseren Breiten ist der wissbegierige Bücherskorpion. Mit etwas Glück findet man ihn in Bibliotheken, aber auch unter Baumrinden. Oder in diesem Buch.

The only scorpion in our latitudes is the book scorpion, keen on knowledge. With a little bit of luck you may find it in libraries or underneath the bark of a tree. Or in this book.